Soup Maker Recipe Book UK Cookbook

More Than 120 Delicious and Healthy Soup Maker Recipes with Easy-to-Follow Instructions. Nutritious Soup Recipes to Boost Your Immune System and Nourish the Soul.

Author: Sophia Smith

TABLE OF CONTENTS

How to Master Soup Makers so You Can Make Delicious Soups in an Easy Way 8

Types of Soup Makers 8

Choosing the Right Soup Maker for you 9

Tips for Using Your Soup Maker to Its Highest Potential 12

Secrets to Making Great Soups 14

Understanding Soup Composition..14

Understanding Classifications of Soup...16

Different Soups for Different Seasons 18

Why Eat Seasonally...19

Produce by Seasons 19

Measurement Conversions 21

Traditional British Soups...23

1.   Roasted Cauliflower & Turmeric Soup 23

2.   Creamy Leek & Stilton Soup 26

3.   Creamy Cullen Skink Soup...27

4.   Smoked Haddock Chowder with Sweet Corn..............................28

5.   Easy Tomato Lentil Soup...29

6.   Yummy Cock – a – Leekie Soup..30

7.   Spicy Carrot & Ginger Soup..31

8.   Vegetable & Bean Soup...32

Bean Soups 33

9.   Split Pea Bacon Soup 34

10.   Butter Bean Soup...35

11.   Healthy Red Split Pea Soup..36

12.   Split pea Mix Vegetable Soup...37

13.   Indian Split Pea Soup..38

14.   Yellow Split Pea Soup 39

15. Spicy Split Pea Carrot Soup..40

16. Flavourful Split pea Carrot Soup 41

17. Nutritious Black Bean Soup 42

18. Red Bean Tomato Soup 43

19. Easy Carrot Green Bean Soup 44

20. Butter Bean Carrot Soup 45

21. Kale Bean Soup 46

22. Chickpea Bean Soup 47

23. Split pea Squash Carrot Soup 48

24. Parsnip Beans Soup 49

25. Apple Potato Leek Soup 50

26. Thick & Creamy Pea Soup 51

27. Easy Mint Pea Soup 52

28. Healthy Chickpea Split Pea Soup 53

Fruity Soups 54

29. Apple Pumpkin Soup 55

30. Squash Pear Soup 56

31. Apple Ginger Squash Soup 57

32. Apple Parsnip Soup 58

33. Cinnamon Squash Apple Soup 59

34. Celery Pear Soup 60

35. Pear Parsnip Soup 61

36. Chili Squash & Pear Soup 62

37. Chunky Apple Carrot Soup 63

Tomato Soups 64

38. Tomato Cabbage Soup 65

39. Flavourful Tomato Soup 66

40. Creamy Tomato Soup 67

41. Parmesan Basil Tomato Soup 68

42. Tomato Spinach Soup 69

43. Easy Carrot Tomato Soup 70

44. Healthy & Easy Tomato Soup..71

45. Roasted Pepper Tomato Soup..72

46. Roasted Eggplant Tomato Soup..73

47. Artichoke Tomato Soup...74

48. Herb Tomato Artichoke Soup..75

49. Tomato Zucchini Soup...76

Root Vegetable Based Soups...77

50. Cabbage Potato Soup..78

51. Creamy Squash Sweet Potato Soup..79

52. Vegan Potato Soup..80

53. Creamy Leek Potato Soup...81

54. Creamy Potato Soup..82

55. Spicy Sweet Potato Soup..83

56. Root Vegetable Soup...84

57. Healthy Celeriac Soup...85

Chunky Vegetable Based Soups...86

58. Pasta Vegetable Soup..87

59. Flavourful Orzo Soup..88

60. Bean Veggie Minestrone Soup..89

61. Broccoli Lemon Soup..90

62. Lime Sweet Corn Soup..91

63. Corn Veg Soup...92

64. Mexican Corn Soup...93

65. Spicy Cabbage Soup..94

66. Cheesy Broccoli Soup..95

67. Cauliflower Broccoli Carrot Soup..96

68. Spicy Pumpkin Soup...97

69. Chunky Broccoli Pumpkin Soup...98

Smooth Vegetable Based Soups...99

70. Creamy Mushroom Soup..100

71. Cheese Broccoli Soup...101

72. Leek Mushroom Soup...102

73. Creamy Mushroom Onion Soup...103

74. Simple Courgette Leek Soup..104

75. Zucchini Coconut Soup 105

76. Cheesy Spinach Soup...106

77. Healthy Spinach Soup..107

78. Almond Asparagus Soup...108

79. Celery Soup 109

80. Caprese Soup 110

81. Vegan Kale Miso Soup 111

82. Versatile Vegetable Soup 112

83. Garlic Corn Soup...113

84. Lebanese Eggplant Soup 114

85. Poblano Corn Soup..115

86. Nutmeg Pumpkin Soup 116

87. Cauliflower Cheese Soup 117

88. Avocado Soup 118

89. Almond Broccoli Cheese Soup 119

90. Roasted Pepper Soup...120

91. Creamy Cauliflower Soup 121

92. Coconut Garlic Mushroom Soup 122

93. Cabbage Coconut Soup...123

94. Broccoli Avocado Soup 124

Soups Made from Poultry 125

95. Chicken Bean Soup..126

96. Red Bean Turkey Soup...127

97. Classic Chicken Noodle Soup...128

98. Tasty Chicken Vegetable Soup...129

99. Chili Chicken Soup..130

100. Chicken Mushroom Soup 131

101. Turkey Bean Soup 132

102. Thai Chicken Soup 133

103. Chicken Sweet corn Soup 134

104. Delicious Asian Chicken Soup 135

105. Cauliflower Chicken Soup 136

106. Chicken Taco Soup 137

Soups Made from Seafood 138

107. Asian Prawn Soup 139

108. Smoked Salmon Cabbage Soup 140

109. Delicious Haddock Minestrone Soup 141

110. Smoked Cod Potato Soup 142

111. Curried Cod Cauliflower Soup 143

112. Haddock Asparagus Soup 144

113. Spinach Cod Soup 145

114. Curried Zucchini & Salmon Soup 146

Ham & Bacon Soups 147

115. Bacon Tomato Soup 148

116. Pea Bacon Soup 149

117. Easy Ham & Broccoli Soup 150

118. Parmesan Bacon Asparagus Soup 151

119. Brussels Sprouts Cauliflower Soup with Bacon Bits 152

120. Creamy Bacon Carrot Sprout Soup 153

121. Blue Cheese, Brussels Sprout & Ham Soup 154

122. Cheesy Bacon Cauliflower Soup 155

Conclusion 156

How to Master Soup Makers so You Can Make Delicious Soups in an Easy Way

If you are seeking a delicious meal that is easy to whip up and perfect for any time of the year, then you need to consider investing in a Soup Maker. Whether you need a quick meal for lunch or something to warm up your kitchen during cold seasons, a good bowl of soup will never let you down. What's even better is that soups can become healthy delicious starters, great main course options with if you have a larger portion or even a light 'pick me up' on a chilly day.

Types of Soup Makers

Before you can completely master a soup maker, you will need to understand the general info of a soup maker, what it looks like, how to use it and how to maintain the appliance. There are essentially two main types of soup makers, each of which appeals to a different subset of people. The first type is essentially a super kettle. They are for people who prefer to keep their appliances basic and simple. These models typically require you to chop your ingredients before tossing them all in your Soup Maker and pressing a button to create delicious soups or smoothies. You will find that even with the need to pre-prep your ingredients it's still a pretty simple process. The second type of Soup Maker is a tad more sophisticated. It is primarily a blender with several functions and whilst this device will still save you time while cooking and cleaning, but they do require more input and if you have less time to invest or are new to soup makers achieving the proper soup consistency without standing over the appliance may be a tad harder than the other model.When it comes to purchasing a soup maker there are other factors that you may want to consider such as weight, appearance, and size. The basic models take up less space and are normally lighter whereas the more versatile soup maker models are larger and a lot heavier particularly if they have a glass jug. You will also need to consider whether you purchase a model that has either a glass, plastic, or stainless jug. The benefit you have when using a plastic or glass jug is that you can see how your cooking is progressing whereas the stainless-steel jug does not give you this option. I would suggest that you look for a model with a timer even if it is basic a this is another good indication to check on the cooking process.

Choosing the Right Soup Maker for you

Once you have made the decision to purchase a soup maker, you will notice that there are many to choose from and that it is worth taking the time to find the one that is fit for you and what you are planning to use it for. All soup makers will ideally provide you with a completed bowl of soup however there are more than one way of getting there! There are soup makers that start from just £35 and those that will cost upwards of £100 and obviously there are varying degrees of quality.

There are some soup makers that can offer you various functions complete with different settings to create soup of various textures and consistencies. There are others that are basic offering a blending and boiling or offer only a minor function when it comes to textures and consistencies. There are machines that are fast and high powered whilst others may take a little longer and must work harder to cook the soup. Some soup makers have superb build quality whilst the cheaper ones can be less sturdy. When you look at reviews there are some soup makers that will have rave reviews whereas others may have a minimal following.

The reason for adding this to the book is to try and provide the various amount of information so that you can make the right choice that will work for you. Although there are many soup makers that will look the same, there is information that differentiates them from each other and if you know what is on offer you should be able to make the right choice for you.

Other features you may want to consider includes:

Power:
This will determine how powerful the appliance will chop and blend. Generally, a more powerful motor may see better results but not always! Also, a more powerful machine may heat up your soup quicker.

Size:
Soup makers have different capacities depending on the quantity of soup you need to make. They generally range from 1.0 to 1.7 litres. Make your choice of capacity dependent on your needs but remember that you can freeze soup so any extras can be used for another meal.

Soups Consistency:
When it comes to choosing the right soup maker for you, you will want to choose a model that gives you many options as this will make it far easier for you when you

are making your soup. The most basic of soup makers tend to only offer two functions, this being either chunky or smooth. If you are seeking a good range of options to choose from when you go to make your soup. If you are intending to be more creative with your soups it would be best for you to find a soup maker that provides you with more choices.

There are soup makers for sale that allow you to control the soup making process whilst it is cooking. The additional features may include a pulse button, additional buttons that let you mix the soup and if you find that you are not happy with the soup you are making you can even alter the soup mid-way through the cooking process.

It may be that you feel you need more power, and if this is the case my advice would be to look for the soup maker that offers you the extra functions and features. However, if you are happy to just switch your soup maker on, press the button and let it do the job, then you should find that a basic model will be right for you.

Non-stick Heating Feature:
Most appliances will advertise this as a feature. You will no doubt know from your own experience that ingredients can sometimes stick and can be stubborn to remove afterwards. Make sure you carefully read reviews of the product before purchasing and follow manufacturer's guidelines for use.

Maintenance:

Whilst using a soup maker certainly reduces the washing up, the unit itself does still need to be cleaned afterwards. Some appliances are easier to clean than others. Research how easily blades, and elements of the unit can be removed for cleaning and again pay attention to reviews of those who have already purchased.

Settings:

There should be multiple heating settings. Usually low, medium, high and simmer. Depending on which model you have you will also have a timer or pre-programmed settings.

The Ability to Stir While Cooking:

This is a handy addition which allows the soup to be stirred by the appliance at regular intervals and can prevent sticking.

Design:

There are some people that put style as their top priority and will therefore be looking for a machine that fits in with their kitchen and décor. There are soup makers that come in beautiful colors, good looking, look expensive and, on the other end of the scale there are ones that you could easily mistake for a standard blender. However, this is not always defined by the price. You will see that soup makers do vary, and therefore it is so important for you to look at all the options and find the one that suits you and your kitchen best. If you find that function is more important to you over style, you can forget about this and focus on other things in your search.

So, if you are not bothered about the appearance of your soup maker looks like you may want to consider the quality of the design. The various models of soup maker that are on offer are created from various materials and some will be more rugged than others and the jug body can be made from plastic or glass. The base of the appliance could be stainless steel or something altogether different so this needs to be a consideration in your decision. Regardless of what the soup maker looks like, a better quality of build could see you purchase an appliance that is more reliable and will last you a lot longer.

Tips for Using Your Soup Maker to Its Highest Potential

Using Soup Makers can be a hit or miss depending on how you use and care for the appliance. Luckily, there are a few methods you can employ that will help you get the most out of your Soup Maker and these include:

- Avoid using use raw meat or seafood, instead use pre-cooked proteins.
- Use hot stock in recipes, not cold.
- Do not overfill your appliance. Pay careful attention to the capacity of your machine and the fill level markers. There are different levels for cold and hot liquids.
- Do not use any meat with bones in the soup maker
- Read the manufactures instructions and guidelines for your appliance thoroughly before using. These will provide information, tips and safety guidelines specific to your product and should be adhered to in order to get the best out of your appliance.
- Always make sure the lid is tightly closed and fastened before cooking.
- Do not use any seafood which are still in their shells in the soup maker
- Be careful of fully immersing your jug in water as this may result in short-circuiting the machine.
- Follow the manufacturer's safety guidelines when using the appliance, particularly when opening the lid after or during cooking, which may release scalding steam.
- Cut your ingredients into small bite size pieces before adding to the soup maker.
- If fitted, use the stir function regularly.
- Prepare all your ingredients first.
- Allow any frozen ingredients to thaw first.
- Do not use frozen ingredients as this will increase cooking times.
- To prevent sticking use a little oil when sautéing.

- Most soup makers are not dishwasher safe so must be cleaned manually. Warm soapy water should be sufficient. If the heating plate has become burned, soak in hot soapy water for longer and use a coarse sponge to remove. Avoid using any harsh cleaning products or scouring pads, as these will damage the surface of the heating plate.
- Allow the soup maker to fully cool before attempting to clean. Heating plates and blades may still be extremely hot.

Secrets to Making Great Soups

What I am about to tell you is going to blow your mind. The secret to making great soups is simply understanding the different classifications and components that make a delicious bowl of soup. If you can master soup composition, you will easily be able to spin just about any meat or vegetable into a delicious bowl of soup.

Understanding Soup Composition

There are three main parts of a good bowl of soup. These are:
1. The base (liquid part of your soup)
2. The main ingredient (whether it's a vegetable or meat), and
3. Your preferred spices or aromatics.

Now that you know the three parts of the soup. Let's examine each separately to give you a better idea.

The Base

Broth made from chicken, meat, or vegetable is used as a base for most soups. Other ingredients include plain water, milk or cream, fish stock, and tomato puree. The quality of the broth or any other cooking liquid you use greatly determines the quality of your soup.

Main Ingredient

The main ingredient you choose should mesh well with the liquid part of your soup. For example, fish stock may not mesh well with a chicken soup.

Spices & Aromatics

Spices and aromatic vegetables are the miracle workers! Onions and garlic are one of the key ingredients to a flavourful, soothing soup. It's worthwhile to sauté onions and garlic until lightly browned or transparent, these releases their flavours. If your Soup Maker doesn't have the sauté function, use a small skillet over a stove pot. Be careful not to burn garlic. It'll ruin your soup. I normally first sauté onions for 3 to 5 minutes, then add garlic for the last one minute or 30 seconds.

Spices determine how your soup will taste. You can use thyme, parsley, chili powder, rosemary, oregano, basil, and other spices. If you are craving for an Indian flavour, turmeric, garam masala, coriander, cumin may help you achieve that taste. For Thai flavour you may want to use ginger, garlic, and ground coriander. Feel free to try different combinations of spices to know which one tickles your taste buds.

Salt and freshly ground black pepper is a constant in my soups. Spices don't eliminate the need for a pinch of sea salt.
As you make the soups in this book, you'll get a clear picture of how broth or stock combines with veggies or meat and spices to make you a perfect soup.
Do you want a chunky, creamy, or smooth soup? You decide whether to blend or not. Whenever I don't want to blend the soup, I cut veggies or meat into small pieces.

Once your soup is ready, finish it beautifully with freshly chopped herbs, finely sliced spring onions, or your favourite garnish.

Understanding Classifications of Soup

There are two main category divisions for soups; these are:

1. Clear (Unthickened) Soups
2. Thick Soups

Clear Soups

As the name suggests, these soups are all based on an unthickened, clear stock or broth. They can be served as is or garnished with a mixture of meats and/or vegetables. This classification can be broken down into further subcategories including:

- *Bouillon and Broths*

These two terms are often used in many different ways. In general terms, however, when used they refer to simple, clear soups that have no solid ingredients outside of the garnish. As discussed above, a broth is a flavourful liquid derived from simmering vegetables or meats.

- *Consommé*

This is essentially a rich, flavourful stock that has been clarified to make it perfectly transparent. These create a brilliant aesthetic for weddings, and restaurant settings. They are also very rich making them perfect for people who have been instructed to follow a clear diet.

- *Vegetable Soups*

Under the clear soup category, a vegetable soup refers to a well-seasoned broth served with produce.

Thick Soups

Thick soups, on the other hand, are mostly opaque. They are thickened either with a roux (thickening agent) or by pureeing one or more ingredients to give it a heavier consistency. This category can be further broken down into subcategories such as:

- *Puree Soups:*

These soups are thickened naturally by pureeing one or more of their ingredients. They are usually made of starchy vegetables such as potatoes, starchy foods such as rice or legumes such as split peas. They may also contain milk or cream, but they are often not as smooth as creamed soups.

- *Cream Soup:*

These soups are thickened with Beurre Manie, roux, liaison or other thickening agents, plus cream or milk. They are often compared to bechamel or velouté sauces and can even be made by diluting then flavouring these lead sauces. These are generally named based on their main ingredient. For example, a cream soup made of onions is called Cream of Onion Soup.

- *Chowders:*

These are hearty soups typically made from vegetables, shellfish or fish. They can be made in many ways but generally contain potatoes or milk.

- *Bisques:*

These soups are thickened soups that are made from shellfish. You generally prepare them as you would a regular soup then finish them with cream.

Different Soups for Different Seasons

People think that eating seasonally is very intimidating and hard to do, but I promise you it's super simple. Here are a few tips to assist in making it easier for you.

My first tip is going to your local farmer's market. Everything there is gonna be grown by the farmers locally so therefore will be in season. Or even if you don't like to shop at your farmers market, you could go take notes of what the farmers have there and then you could buy those things at your grocery store.
The second tip is at your grocery store take a note of what there is a lot of right now.

I know in my grocery store there is a lot of squash, there is a lot of apples, there's a lot of greens, so I know all of those things are in season. And the second thing is to look for what is on sale. What is in season is often gonna be on sale. It is simple supply and demand. There is a lot being grown by the farmers and a lot that they need to sell, so prices go down.

There are often signs in your grocery store that tell you where the food is grown from so if the food is being grown somewhere relatively close to you, it probably means it is in season. If they're having to ship it from pretty far away, probably means that it's not in your local season. So, I would stay away from those things. So those are three good things to check when you're in the grocery store to help know what's in season.

Why Eat Seasonally

If you aren't already convinced, here are a few reasons you should considered eating seasonally:

1. It helps local farmers.
2. It helps continue the cycle of supply and demand. Farmers have a lot of it so if people consume it, it works out really well.
3. Prices are often lower because there are often a lot available.
4. Eating seasonally can actually help you figure out what pairs well together. Often what's grown in season together, pairs really well in recipes.

Produce by Seasons

Spring

Spinach	Turnips	Mushrooms
Collard Greens	Kale	Rhubarb
Swiss Chard	Onions	Strawberries
Bananas	Limes	Broccoli
Avocados	Garlic	Asparagus
Radishes	Apples	Kiwifruit
Lemons	Celery	Peas
Lettuce	Carrots	Pineapples
Apricots	Cabbage	

Summer

Honeydew Melon	Carrots	Blueberries
Summer Squash	Garlic	Apricots
Apples	Strawberries	Celery
Green Beans	Corn	Cantaloupe
Tomatillos	Lima Beans	Peaches
Blackberries	Avocados	Raspberries
Plums	Watermelon	Cherries
Eggplant	Lemons	Okra
Limes	Zucchini	Tomatoes
Cucumbers	Bananas	Mangos
Bell Peppers	Beets	

Autumn/Fall

Onions
Collard Greens
Grapes
Celery
Sweet Potatoes & Yams
Lemons
Green Beans
Pineapples
Pumpkin
Swiss Chard
Limes
Radishes

Peas
Bell Peppers
Cauliflower
Kiwifruit
Apples
Beets
Bananas
Raspberries
Parsnips
Turnips
Carrots
Pears
Mangos

Brussels Sprouts
Winter Squash
Potatoes
Ginger
Cranberries
Spinach
Cabbage
Garlic
Lettuce
Kale
Rutabagas
Mushrooms
Broccoli

Winter

Grapefruit
Collard Greens
Avocados
Brussels Sprouts
Leeks
Celery
Parsnips
Sweet Potatoes & Yams
Bananas

Apples
Pumpkin
Lemons
Potatoes
Pears
Winter Squash
Carrots
Swiss Chard
Limes
Oranges

Onions
Beets
Kale
Turnips
Pineapples
Kiwifruit
Cabbage
Rutabagas

Measurement Conversions

It is important to note that it is virtually impossible to include an all-inclusive conversion table as all foods have slightly different measurements when converted.

KITCHEN CONVERSIONS

LIQUID CONVERSIONS

1/4 TSP	=	1 ML				
1/2 TSP	=	2 ML				
1 TSP	=	5 ML				
3 TSP	=	1 TBL	= 1/2 FL OZ	= 15 ML		
2 TBLS	=	1/8 CUP	= 1 FL OZ	= 30 ML		
4 TBLS	=	1/4 CUP	= 2 FL OZ	= 60 ML		
5 1/3 TBLS	=	1/3 CUP	= 3 FL OZ	= 80 ML		
8 TBLS	=	1/2 CUP	= 4 FL OZ	= 120 ML		
10 2/3	=	2/3 CUP	= 5 FL OZ	= 160 ML		
12 TBLS	=	3/4 CUP	= 6 FL OZ	= 180 ML		
16 TBLS	=	1 CUP	= 8 FL OZ	= 240 ML		
1 PT	=	2 CUPS	= 16 FL OZ	= 480 ML		
1 QT	=	4 CUPS	= 32 FL OZ	= 960 ML		
33 FL OZ	=	1000 ML	= 1 L			

Length

METRIC	IMPERIAL
3mm	1/8 inch
6mm	1/4 inch
2.5cm	1 inch
3cm	1 1/4 inch
5cm	2 inches
10cm	4 inches
15cm	6 inches
20cm	8 inches
22.5cm	9 inches
25cm	10 inches
28cm	11 inches

Oven Temperatures

	Fahrenheit	Celsius	Gas Mark
Freezing Water	32°F	0°C	
Room Temp.	68°F	20°C	
Boiling Water	212° F	100°C	
Baking	325° F	160°C	3
	350° F	180°C	4
	375° F	190°C	5
	400° F	200°C	6
	425° F	220°C	7
	450° F	230°C	8
Broiling			Grill

Weight Conversions

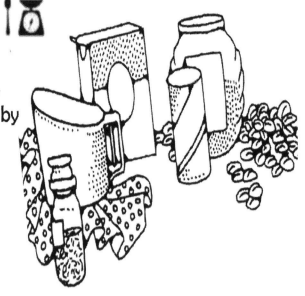

(To convert ounces to grams, multiply the number of ounces by 30.)

1 oz	=	1/16 lb	=	30 g
4 oz	=	1/4 lb	=	120 g
8 oz	=	1/2 lb	=	240 g
12 oz	=	3/4 lb	=	360 g
16 oz	=	1 lb	=	480 g

Conversions for Different Types of Food

Standard Cup	Fine Powder (like flour)	Grains (like rice)	Granular (like sugar)	Liquid Solids (like butter)	Liquid (eg. milk)
1	140 g	150 g	190 g	200 g	240 ml
3/4	105 g	113 g	143 g	150 g	180 ml
2/3	93 g	100 g	125 g	133 g	160 ml
1/2	70 g	75 g	95 g	100 g	120 ml
1/3	47 g	50 g	63 g	67 g	80 ml
1/4	35 g	38 g	48 g	50 g	60 ml
1/8	18 g	19 g	24 g	25 g	30 ml

Before I share all the recipes, I would just like to thank you for your trust and I really hope you'll enjoy the recipes.

A lot of thought and effort went into creating so many recipes. I am not a part of a big publishing company and I take care of the whole publishing process myself in an effort to make sure your bellies are satisfied with the recipes provided.

If for any reason you did not like the book you can write on my email at deliciousrecipes.publishing@gmail.com. I always make sure to get back to everybody and if you are not happy with the recipes I can share another cookbook or two for free.

I'm trying really hard to create the best cookbooks I can, and I'm always open to constructive criticism.

Enjoy the recipes!

Traditional British Soups

Roasted Cauliflower & Turmeric Soup

Servings|6   Time|30 minutes
Nutritional Content (per serving):
Cal| 76   Fat| 2g   Protein| 4g   Carbs| 12g

Ingredients:

- ❖ 1 medium cauliflower head, cut into florets, roasted
- ❖ 3g dried parsley
- ❖ ½ carrot, peeled and chopped
- ❖ 9.86 g. turmeric powder
- ❖ ½ celery, peeled and chopped
- ❖ 3g dried mix herbs
- ❖ 240 ml of water
- ❖ 65 ml yogurt
- ❖ 1 bell pepper
- ❖ 1 small butternut squash, peeled and chopped
- ❖ 1 onion, chopped
- ❖ Pepper
- ❖ Salt

Directions:

1. Add all ingredients except yogurt into the soup maker. Seal soup maker with lid and cook for 25 minutes on blend mode.
2. Add yogurt and stir well. Season soup with salt and pepper. Serve and enjoy.

Creamy Leek & Stilton Soup

Servings|4   Time|30 minutes
Nutritional Content (per serving):
Cal| 136   Fat| 3.2g   Protein| 3.2g   Carbs| 24.9g

Ingredients:

- ❖ 2 leeks, sliced
- ❖ 950 ml vegetable stock
- ❖ 5 g garlic, minced
- ❖ 1 onion, chopped
- ❖ 340 g. potato, peeled and diced
- ❖ 14 g butter
- ❖ 230 g Stilton cheese
- ❖ Pepper
- ❖ Salt

Directions:

1. Melt butter in a saucepan over medium heat. Add onion and sauté for 2 minutes.
2. Add garlic and leek and sauté for 2-3 minutes or until leek is softened. Transfer sautéed onion, garlic, and leek to the soup maker.
3. Add remaining ingredients and stir well. Seal soup maker with lid and cook on smooth mode. Season soup with salt and pepper. Serve and enjoy.

Creamy Cullen Skink Soup

Servings|4   Time|32 minutes
Nutritional Content (per serving):
Cal| 313   Fat| 10g   Protein| 26g   Carbs| 30g

Ingredients:

- ❖ 450 g. haddock, smoked fillets, diced
- ❖ 600 ml milk
- ❖ 2 celery stalks, sliced
- ❖ 1 bay leaf
- ❖ 1 onion, diced

- ❖ 2 medium potatoes, peeled, cooked mashed
- ❖ 55 g butter
- ❖ Pepper
- ❖ Salt
- ❖ Parsley (a handful, for garnish)

Directions:

1. Transfer all your ingredients, except the bay leaf to the soup maker and stir well.
2. Seal soup maker with lid and cook on smooth mode.
3. When done, switch off the Soup Maker, add in bay leaf, and cover. Allow bay leaf to be infused for about 5 minutes.
4. Discard bay leaf. Season soup with salt and pepper. Serve and enjoy.

Smoked Haddock Chowder with Sweet Corn

Servings|4   Time|32 minutes
Nutritional Content (per serving):
Cal| 313   Fat| 10g   Protein| 26g   Carbs| 30g

Ingredients:

- ❖ 340 g haddock, smoked fillets, undyed, diced
- ❖ 591 ml. milk
- ❖ 2 leeks, cleaned and trimmed, diced
- ❖ 1 bay leaf
- ❖ ½ carrot, peeled and diced
- ❖ 1 onion, diced
- ❖ 16 g flour, all-purpose
- ❖ 2 medium potatoes, peeled, cooked mashed
- ❖ 56 g butter
- ❖ 30 g baby spinach, leaves only, shredded
- ❖ 177 ml heavy cream (or double cream)
- ❖ 120 g sweet corn, canned
- ❖ Pepper
- ❖ Salt
- ❖ 14 g Parsley (flat leaf)

Directions:

1. Transfer all your ingredients, except the bay leaf and sweet corn to the soup maker and stir well.
2. Seal soup maker with lid and cook on smooth mode.
3. When done, switch off the Soup Maker, stir in bay leaf and sweet corn.
4. Cover and allow to sit so the bay leaf can be infused for about 5 minutes.
5. Discard bay leaf. Season soup with salt and pepper. Serve and enjoy.

Easy Tomato Lentil Soup

Servings|6   Time|26 minutes
Nutritional Content (per serving):
Cal| 161   Fat| 1g   Protein| 9.2g   Carbs| 36g

Ingredients:

- ❖ 95 g red lentils, rinsed and soaked in water for 30 minutes
- ❖ 2 g dried mix herbs
- ❖ 1 vegetable stock cube
- ❖ 30 g tomato puree
- ❖ 1 large carrot, chopped
- ❖ 3 g garlic, sliced
- ❖ 1 large onion, chopped
- ❖ 5 large tomatoes, chopped
- ❖ 960 ml of water
- ❖ Pepper
- ❖ Salt

Directions:

1. Add all ingredients into the soup maker and stir well. Seal soup maker with lid and cook on smooth mode.
2. Season soup with salt and pepper. Serve and enjoy.

Yummy Cock – a – Leekie Soup

Servings|6   Time|33 minutes
Nutritional Content (per serving):
Cal| 116   Fat| 2g   Protein| 13g   Carbs| 11g

Ingredients:

- ❖ 230 g chicken, cooked and shredded
- ❖ 12 medium leeks, cleaned, trimmed, chopped
- ❖ 1 chicken stock cube
- ❖ 110 g rice, long grain, washed
- ❖ 950 ml chicken stock
- ❖ 4 medium carrots, peeled, grated
- ❖ Pepper
- ❖ Salt

Directions:

1. Add all ingredients into the soup maker and stir well.
2. Seal soup maker with lid and cook on chunky mode for 28 minutes.
3. Season soup with salt and pepper. Serve and enjoy.

Spicy Carrot & Ginger Soup

Servings|4   Time|40 minutes
Nutritional Content (per serving):
Cal| 226   Fat|8g   Protein| 9g   Carbs| 34g

Ingredients:

- ❖ 680 g carrots, peeled and chopped
- ❖ 2 cloves garlic, crushed
- ❖ 8 g ginger, ground
- ❖ 15 ml olive oil
- ❖ 950 ml chicken broth
- ❖ 15 ml lemon juice
- ❖ 1 onion, chopped
- ❖ Pepper
- ❖ Salt

Directions:

1. Heat oil in a pan over medium heat. Add onion and garlic and sauté until onion is softened. Transfer to the soup maker.
2. Add remaining ingredients to the soup maker and stir well. Seal soup maker with lid and cook on smooth mode for 21 minutes.
3. Season soup with salt and pepper. Serve and enjoy.

Vegetable & Bean Soup

Servings|4   Time|40 minutes
Nutritional Content (per serving):
Cal| 381   Fat| 13g   Protein| 16g   Carbs|54g

Ingredients:

- ❖ 360 g white beans, rinsed
- ❖ 1 litre vegetable stock
- ❖ 3 garlic cloves, minced
- ❖ 2 celery stalks, diced
- ❖ 1 onion, chopped
- ❖ 1 g dried thyme
- ❖ 4 g sugar
- ❖ 1 bay leaf
- ❖ 2 oz. butter
- ❖ salt and pepper

Directions:

1. Melt butter in a pan over medium heat. Add carrots, celery, and onion sauté until softened, about 5 minutes. Add garlic and sauté for a minute. Transfer to the soup maker.
2. Add remaining ingredients to the soup maker and stir well. Seal soup maker with lid and cook on chunky mode for 28 minutes.
3. Discard bay leaf. Serve and enjoy.

Bean Soups

Split Pea Bacon Soup

Servings|4   Time|25 minutes
Nutritional Content (per serving):
Cal| 332   Fat| 10g   Protein| 20g   Carbs| 41g

Ingredients:

- 950 ml vegetable stock
- 45 g. carrot, chopped
- 1 potato, peeled and chopped
- 200 g split red split peas, rinsed
- 26 g onion, chopped
- 3 bacon slices, chopped
- 15 ml olive oil
- Pepper
- Salt

Directions:

1. Heat oil in a pan over medium heat. Add onion and bacon and sauté for 3-4 minutes. Transfer sautéed onion and bacon to the soup maker.
2. Add remaining ingredients and stir well. Seal soup maker with lid and cook on smooth mode. Season soup with salt and pepper. Serve and enjoy.

Butter Bean Soup

Servings|4   Time|30 minutes
Nutritional Content (per serving):
Cal| 240   Fat| 5g   Protein| 13.2g   Carbs| 36g

Ingredients:

- 400 g can butter beans
- 766 ml vegetable stock
- 0.85 g coriander powder
- 280 g passata
- 1 ⅛ dl split red split peas, rinsed
- 1.4 g garlic, crushed
- 1 medium onion, chopped
- 15 ml olive oil
- Pepper
- Salt

Directions:

1. Heat oil in a pan over medium heat. Add onion and sauté until softened. Add garlic and sauté for 30 seconds. Transfer sautéed onion and garlic to the soup maker.
2. Add remaining ingredients and stir well. Seal soup maker with lid and cook on smooth mode. Season soup with salt and pepper. Serve and enjoy.

Healthy Red Split Pea Soup

Servings|4   Time|26 minutes
Nutritional Content (per serving):
Cal| 382   Fat| 1.2g   Protein| 26g   Carbs| 67g

Ingredients:

- ❖ 250 g. split red split peas, rinsed and soaked in water for 30 minutes
- ❖ 1 medium onion, chopped
- ❖ 950 ml vegetable stock
- ❖ 140 g potatoes, peeled and diced
- ❖ Pepper
- ❖ Salt

Directions:
1. Add all ingredients into the soup maker and stir well. Seal soup maker with lid and cook on smooth mode.
2. Season soup with salt and pepper. Serve and enjoy.

Split Pea Mix Vegetable Soup

Servings|4   Time|30 minutes
Nutritional Content (per serving):
Cal| 89   Fat| 1g   Protein| 5g   Carbs| 16g

Ingredients:

- ❖ 450 g mixed vegetables, chopped
- ❖ 765 ml vegetable stock
- ❖ 2 g garlic, minced
- ❖ 55 g split peas
- ❖ 50 g allspice mix
- ❖ Pepper
- ❖ Salt

Directions:

1. Add all ingredients into the soup maker and stir well. Seal soup maker with lid and cook on smooth mode. Season soup with salt and pepper.
2. Serve and enjoy.

Indian Split Pea Soup

Servings|5   Time|26 minutes
Nutritional Content (per serving):
Cal| 120   Fat| 1g   Protein| 8g   Carbs| 21g

Ingredients:

- ❖ 170 g red split peas, rinsed and soaked in water for 30 minutes
- ❖ 1 vegetable bouillon cube
- ❖ 1 red chili, chopped
- ❖ 150 g cherry tomatoes
- ❖ 1 carrot, peeled and chopped
- ❖ 5 g fresh ginger, minced
- ❖ 3 g garlic, minced
- ❖ Pepper
- ❖ Salt

Directions:

1. Add all ingredients into the soup maker. Add water to the soup maker up to the max mark. Seal soup maker with lid and cook on smooth mode.
2. Season soup with salt and pepper. Serve and enjoy.

Yellow Split Pea Soup

Servings|5   Time|26 minutes
Nutritional Content (per serving):
Cal| 180   Fat| 1g   Protein| 12g   Carbs| 32g

Ingredients:

- ❖ 225g split yellow split peas, rinsed and soaked in water for 1 hour
- ❖ 250 ml water
- ❖ 2 g oregano
- ❖ 3g chili powder
- ❖ 10g ginger garlic paste
- ❖ 1 medium onion, chopped
- ❖ 1 large carrot, peeled and chopped
- ❖ 14 oz can tomato
- ❖ Pepper
- ❖ Salt

Directions:
1. Add all ingredients into the soup maker and stir well. Seal soup maker with lid and cook on smooth mode.
2. Season soup with salt and pepper. Serve and enjoy.

Spicy Split Pea Carrot Soup

Servings|4   Time|26 minutes
Nutritional Content (per serving):
Cal| 238   Fat| 5g   Protein| 12g   Carbs| 38g

Ingredients:

- ❖ 570 g carrots, peeled and chopped
- ❖ 120 ml milk
- ❖ 2 vegetable stock cubes
- ❖ 960 ml of water
- ❖ 170 g red split peas, rinsed and soaked in water for 30 minutes
- ❖ 3 g cumin seeds
- ❖ 1 g red chili flakes
- ❖ 15 ml olive oil

Directions:

1. Heat oil in a pan over medium heat. Once the oil is hot, add cumin seeds and red chili flakes and fry until cumin seeds crackle.
2. Add carrots into the pan and stir everything well. Transfer to the soup maker.
3. Add remaining ingredients to the soup maker and stir well. Seal soup maker with lid and cook on smooth mode.
4. Season soup with salt and pepper. Serve and enjoy.

Flavourful Split pea Carrot Soup

Servings|4   Time|26minutes
Nutritional Content (per serving):
Cal| 248   Fat| 1g   Protein| 16g   Carbs| 44g

Ingredients:

- ❖ 230 g red split peas, rinsed and soaked in water for 30 minutes
- ❖ 15 ml fresh lemon juice
- ❖ 10 g fresh coriander, chopped
- ❖ 1 onion, chopped
- ❖ 1 sweet red pepper, chopped
- ❖ 2 large carrots, peeled and chopped
- ❖ 2 g paprika
- ❖ 1 g coriander powder
- ❖ 2 g cumin powder
- ❖ 3g garlic, minced
- ❖ 950 ml vegetable stock
- ❖ Pepper
- ❖ Salt

Directions:

1. Add split peas, onion, red pepper, carrots, paprika, coriander powder, cumin powder, garlic, stock, pepper, and salt into the soup maker.
2. Seal soup maker with lid and cook on smooth mode. Add lemon juice and stir well. Season soup with salt and pepper. Garnish with chopped coriander and serve.

Nutritious Black Bean Soup

Servings|4   Time|30 minutes
Nutritional Content (per serving):
Cal| 235   Fat| 4.2g   Protein| 4g   Carbs| 44g

Ingredients:

- ❖ 400 g can black beans
- ❖ 2 sweet potatoes, peeled and chopped
- ❖ 720 ml vegetable stock
- ❖ 1 g cayenne pepper
- ❖ 1 g cumin powder
- ❖ 3 g garlic, minced
- ❖ 1 carrot, peeled and chopped
- ❖ 1 onion, chopped
- ❖ 15 ml olive oil
- ❖ Pepper
- ❖ Salt

Directions:

1. Heat oil in a pan over medium heat. Add onion and sauté for 2 minutes. Add garlic and sauté for 30 seconds.
2. Transfer sautéed onion and garlic to the soup maker.
3. Add remaining ingredients and stir well. Seal soup maker with lid and cook on smooth mode. Season soup with salt and pepper. Serve and enjoy.

Red Bean Tomato Soup

Servings|4   Time|38minutes
Nutritional Content (per serving):
Cal| 169   Fat| 0g   Protein| 8g   Carbs| 33g

Ingredients:

- 400 g can tomato, chopped
- 400 g can kidney beans, rinsed and drained
- 360 ml water
- 50 g wheat bulgur
- 14 g tomato puree
- 2 g paprika
- 1 g dried basil
- 1 onion, diced
- 2 vegetable stock cubes
- 3 g garlic, minced
- Pepper
- Salt

Directions:
1. Add all ingredients into the soup maker and stir well. Seal soup maker with lid and cook on chunky mode.
2. Season soup with salt and pepper. Serve and enjoy.

Easy Carrot Green Bean Soup

Servings|2   Time|33 minutes
Nutritional Content (per serving):
Cal| 84   Fat| 0.2g   Protein| 3.2g   Carbs| 19g

Ingredients:

- ❖ 300 g green beans, diced
- ❖ 300 g carrot, diced
- ❖ 3 g fresh parsley, chopped
- ❖ 250 ml vegetable stock
- ❖ Pepper
- ❖ Salt

Directions:

1. Add all ingredients into the soup maker and stir well. Seal soup maker with lid and cook on chunky mode.
2. Season soup with salt and pepper. Serve and enjoy.

Butter Bean Carrot Soup

Servings|4   Time|26 minutes
Nutritional Content (per serving):
Cal| 159   Fat| 1g   Protein| 7g   Carbs| 31

Ingredients:

- 570 g carrots, peeled and chopped
- 2 g coriander powder
- 2 vegetable stock cubes
- 1 l of water
- 1 onion, chopped
- 400 g can butter beans, rinsed and drained
- Pepper
- Salt

Directions:
1. Add all ingredients into the soup maker and stir well. Seal soup maker with lid and cook on smooth mode. Season soup with salt and pepper. Serve and enjoy.

Kale Bean Soup

Servings|5   Cook Time|30 minutes
Nutritional Content (per serving):
Cal| 156   Fat| 4g   Protein| 6g   Carbs| 25g

Ingredients:

- 135 g kale, tough stalks removed
- 1 l vegetable stock
- 400 g can butter beans, drained and rinsed
- 1 potato, peeled and cubed
- 2 g garlic, minced
- 1 onion, chopped
- 1 leek, chopped
- 15 ml olive oil
- Pepper
- Salt

Directions:

1. Heat oil in a pan over medium heat. Add garlic and onion and sauté for 2-3 minutes. Transfer sautéed garlic and onion to the soup maker.
2. Add remaining ingredients and stir well. Seal soup maker with lid and cook on smooth mode. Season soup with salt and pepper. Serve and enjoy.

Chickpea Bean Soup

Servings|4   Time|30 minutes
Nutritional Content (per serving):
Cal| 223   Fat| 5g   Protein| 9g   Carbs| 38g

Ingredients:

- ❖ 300 g canned chickpeas, rinsed and drained
- ❖ 315 g canned black beans, rinsed and drained
- ❖ 720 ml dl vegetable stock
- ❖ 1/2 bell pepper, diced
- ❖ 1 cumin powder
- ❖ 1 jalapeno pepper, chopped
- ❖ 30 ml fresh lime juice
- ❖ 4 g garlic, minced
- ❖ 1 onion, chopped
- ❖ 15ml olive oil
- ❖ Pepper
- ❖ Salt

Directions:

1. Heat oil in a pan over medium heat. Add onion and garlic and sauté for 2-3 minutes. Transfer sautéed onion and garlic to the soup maker.
2. Add remaining ingredients and stir well. Seal soup maker with lid and cook on smooth mode. Season soup with salt and pepper. Serve and enjoy.

Split pea Squash Carrot Soup

Servings|2   Time|26 minutes
Nutritional Content (per serving):
Cal| 149   Fat| 1g   Protein| 6g   Carbs| 43g

Ingredients:

- ❖ 230 g butternut squash, peeled, deseeded, and chopped
- ❖ 28 g red split peas, rinsed
- ❖ 1 vegetable stock cube
- ❖ 475 ml vegetable stock
- ❖ 2 carrots, peeled and chopped
- ❖ 1 medium onion, chopped
- ❖ Pepper
- ❖ Salt

Directions:

1. Add all ingredients into the soup maker and stir well. Seal soup maker with lid and cook on smooth mode.
2. Season soup with salt and pepper. Serve and enjoy.

Parsnip Beans Soup

Servings|4   Time|1 hour
Nutritional Content (per serving):
Cal| 282   Fat| 5g   Protein| 10g   Carbs| 54g

Ingredients:

- ❖ 570 g parsnips, peeled and quartered
- ❖ 1 celery stick, chopped
- ❖ 2 vegetable stock cubes
- ❖ 150 ml milk
- ❖ 400 g can cannellini beans, rinsed and drained
- ❖ 1 g cumin seeds
- ❖ 1 g turmeric powder
- ❖ 2 g garlic, minced
- ❖ 1 onion, chopped
- ❖ 1 potato, peeled and diced
- ❖ 480 ml of water
- ❖ 15 ml olive oil
- ❖ Pepper
- ❖ Salt

Directions:

1. Preheat the oven to 180 C. Place parsnip, garlic, and onion on a baking tray and drizzle with oil.
2. Season with salt and pepper. Roast in preheated oven for 30 minutes.
3. Transfer roasted parsnip, garlic, and onion to the soup maker. Add remaining ingredients to the soup maker and stir well.
4. Seal soup maker with lid and cook on smooth mode for 21 minutes. Season soup with salt and pepper. Serve and enjoy.

Apple Potato Leek Soup

Servings|4   Time|26 minutes
Nutritional Content (per serving):
Cal| 87   Fat| 1g   Protein| 2g   Carbs| 20g

Ingredients:

- 200 g potato, peeled and chopped
- 2 leeks, sliced
- 120 g apple, diced
- 1 g dried rosemary
- 1 g mustard powder
- 2 g cayenne pepper
- 900 ml water
- 1 garlic clove, peeled
- 2 vegetable stock cubes
- Pepper
- Salt

Directions:

1. Add all ingredients into the soup maker and stir well. Seal soup maker with lid and cook on smooth mode for 21 minutes.
2. Season soup with salt and pepper. Serve and enjoy.

Thick & Creamy Pea Soup

Servings|4   Time|26 minutes
Nutritional Content (per serving):
Cal| 313   Fat| 5g   Protein| 24g   Carbs| 45g

Ingredients:

- ❖ 300 g green split peas, rinsed and soaked overnight
- ❖ 720 ml vegetable stock
- ❖ 180 g ham, cooked and shredded
- ❖ 2 g garlic, crushed
- ❖ 1 onion, chopped
- ❖ Pepper
- ❖ Salt

Directions:

1. Add all ingredients into the soup maker and stir well. Seal soup maker with lid and cook on chunky mode for 21 minutes.
2. Season soup with salt and pepper. Serve and enjoy.

Easy Mint Pea Soup

Servings|4   Time|30 minutes
Nutritional Content (per serving):
Cal| 154   Fat| 1g   Protein| 10g   Carbs| 29g

Ingredients:

- ❖ 600 g frozen peas
- ❖ 90 ml vegetable stock
- ❖ 4 g fresh mint leaves
- ❖ 1 onion, chopped
- ❖ Pepper
- ❖ Salt

Directions:

1. Add all ingredients to the soup maker and stir well. Seal soup maker with lid and cook on smooth mode for 25 minutes.
2. Season soup with salt and pepper. Serve and enjoy.

Healthy Chickpea Split Pea Soup

Servings|6   Time|38 minutes
Nutritional Content (per serving):
Cal| 275   Fat| 6g   Protein| 13g   Carbs| 43g

Ingredients:

- 225 g dry red split peas, rinsed and soaked for 2 hours
- 0.5 g cayenne powder
- 0.5 g coriander powder
- 1 g chili powder
- 0.5 g cinnamon
- 0.5 g paprika
- 0.5 g turmeric
- 30 ml olive oil
- 2 g fresh ginger, minced
- 3 garlic cloves, minced
- 400 g can chickpeas
- 15 ml fresh lemon juice
- 480 ml of water
- 950 ml vegetable stock
- 400 g can tomato, diced
- 128 g carrot, diced
- 150 g onion, diced
- 7 g sea salt

Directions:

1. Heat oil in a pan over medium heat. Add carrots, onion, ginger, and garlic and sauté until onion is softened. Transfer to the soup maker.
2. Add remaining ingredients to the soup maker and stir well. Seal soup maker with lid and cook on chunky mode for 28 minutes. Serve and enjoy.

Fruity Soups

Apple Pumpkin Soup

Servings|4   Time|30 minutes
Nutritional Content (per serving):
Cal| 146   Fat| 8g   Protein| 2g   Carbs| 21g

Ingredients:

- ❖ 120 g green apple, chopped
- ❖ 240 g pumpkin, cubed
- ❖ 1 onion, chopped
- ❖ 3 g garlic, chopped
- ❖ 30 ml olive oil
- ❖ 475 g vegetable stock
- ❖ Pepper
- ❖ Salt

Directions:

1. Heat oil in a pan over medium heat. Add onion and garlic and sauté for 2-3 minutes. Transfer to the soup maker.
2. Add remaining ingredients to the soup maker and stir well. Seal soup maker with lid and cook on smooth mode for 20 minutes.
3. Season soup with salt and pepper. Serve and enjoy.

Squash Pear Soup

Servings|4   Time|30 minutes
Nutritional Content (per serving):
Cal| 256   Fat| 8g   Protein| 4g   Carbs| 50g

Ingredients:

- 910 g butternut squash, roasted and chopped
- 15 ml vinegar
- 712 ml vegetable stock
- 1 g dried sage
- 2 pears, peeled and chopped
- 2 celery, peeled and chopped
- 2 carrots, peeled and chopped
- 3 g garlic, minced
- 1 onion, chopped
- 30 ml olive oil
- Pepper
- Salt

Directions:

1. Heat oil in a pan over medium heat. Add onion and garlic and sauté for 2-3 minutes. Transfer to the soup maker.
2. Add remaining ingredients to the soup maker and stir well. Seal soup maker with lid and cook on smooth mode for 21 minutes.
3. Season soup with salt and pepper. Serve and enjoy.

Apple Ginger Squash Soup

Servings|6   Time|30 minutes
Nutritional Content (per serving):
Cal| 100   Fat| 3g   Protein| 2g   Carbs| 20g

Ingredients:

- ❖ 180 g carrots, chopped
- ❖ 1 L vegetable stock
- ❖ 375 g unsweetened applesauce
- ❖ 1 g cinnamon
- ❖ 2 g curry powder
- ❖ 1g turmeric
- ❖ 2 g garlic, minced
- ❖ 5 g ginger, grated
- ❖ 455 g butternut squash, cubed
- ❖ 1 onion, chopped
- ❖ 15 ml olive oil
- ❖ Salt

Directions:
1. Heat oil in a pan over medium heat. Add onion and garlic and sauté until onion is softened. Transfer to the soup maker.
2. Add remaining ingredients to the soup maker and stir well. Seal soup maker with lid and cook on smooth mode for 21 minutes. Serve and enjoy.

Apple Parsnip Soup

Servings|6   Time|35 minutes
Nutritional Content (per serving):
Cal| 183   Fat| 7g   Protein| 2g   Carbs| 32g

Ingredients:

- ❖ 3 apples, peeled, cored, and chopped
- ❖ 110 ml heavy cream
- ❖ 910 ml vegetable stock
- ❖ 3 g fresh thyme, chopped
- ❖ 450 g parsnips, peeled and chopped
- ❖ 3 g garlic, minced
- ❖ 1 onion, chopped
- ❖ 15 ml tbsp olive oil
- ❖ Pepper
- ❖ Salt

Directions:
1. Heat oil in a pan over medium heat. Add onion and garlic and sauté until onion is softened. Transfer to the soup maker.
2. Add remaining ingredients except for cream to the soup maker and stir well. Seal soup maker with lid and cook on smooth mode for 21 minutes.
3. Add heavy cream and stir well. Season with salt and pepper. Serve and enjoy.

Cinnamon Squash Apple Soup

Servings|6   Time|26 minutes
Nutritional Content (per serving):
Cal| 70   Fat| 0g   Protein| 2g   Carbs| 18g

Ingredients:

- 120 g apple, chopped
- 680 g butternut squash, chopped
- Pinch of nutmeg
- 1 g cinnamon
- 1 bell pepper, chopped
- 1 onion, chopped
- 1.2 L vegetable stock
- Pepper
- Salt

Directions:

1. Add all ingredients into the soup maker and stir well. Seal soup maker with lid and cook on smooth mode for 21 minutes.
2. Season soup with salt and pepper. Serve and enjoy.

Celery Pear Soup

Servings|4   Time|30 minutes
Nutritional Content (per serving):
Cal| 166   Fat| 8g   Protein| 3g   Carbs| 24g

Ingredients:

- 125 g celery stalks, chopped
- 15 ml fresh lemon juice
- 765 ml vegetable stock
- 210 g pears, chopped
- 1 onion, chopped
- 465 g celery root, cubed
- 30 ml olive oil

Directions:

1. Heat oil in a pan over medium heat. Add onion, celery stalks, and celery root and sauté until onion is softened. Transfer to the soup maker.
2. Add remaining ingredients except lemon juice to the soup maker and stir well. Seal soup maker with lid and cook on smooth mode for 21 minutes.
3. Add lemon juice and stir well. Season soup with salt and pepper. Serve and enjoy.

Pear Parsnip Soup

Servings|4   Time|30 minutes
Nutritional Content (per serving):
Cal| 237   Fat| 12g   Protein| 2g   Carbs| 22g

Ingredients:

- 160 g pears, peeled and chopped
- 110 heavy cream
- 1.2 L vegetable stock
- 210 ml dry white wine
- 50 g celery, chopped
- 135 g parsnips, peeled and chopped
- 13 g onion, chopped
- 25 g butter
- Pepper
- Salt

Directions:

1. Melt butter in a pan over medium heat. Add onion and celery and sauté until onion is softened. Transfer to the soup maker.
2. Add remaining ingredients except for heavy cream to the soup maker and stir well. Seal soup maker with lid and cook on smooth mode for 21 minutes.
3. Add heavy cream and stir well. Season with salt and pepper. Serve and enjoy.

Chili Squash & Pear Soup

Servings|4   Time|38 minutes
Nutritional Content (per serving):
Cal| 272   Fat| 22g   Protein| 22g   Carbs| 3g

Ingredients:

- ❖ 450 g butternut squash, diced
- ❖ 1 lime, juiced
- ❖ 235 ml of coconut milk
- ❖ 70 g pears, chopped
- ❖ 765 ml vegetable stock
- ❖ 2 g ginger, grated

- ❖ 1 red chili, sliced
- ❖ 2 g cumin powder
- ❖ 1 onion, chopped
- ❖ 30 ml olive oil
- ❖ Pepper
- ❖ Salt

Directions:

1. Heat oil in a pan over medium heat. Add onion and sauté until softened. Transfer to the soup maker. Add remaining ingredients to the soup maker and stir well.
2. Seal soup maker with lid and cook on chunky mode for 28 minutes. Season soup with salt and pepper. Serve and enjoy.

Chunky Apple Carrot Soup

Servings|4   Time|38 minutes
Nutritional Content (per serving):
Cal| 104   Fat| 0g   Protein| 3g   Carbs| 23

Ingredients:

- ❖ 6 medium apples, diced
- ❖ 1 g thyme
- ❖ 1 medium onion diced
- ❖ 0.5 g dried mixed herbs
- ❖ 2 g chives
- ❖ 30 g yogurt
- ❖ 4 celery sticks, diced
- ❖ 4 medium carrots, peeled and diced
- ❖ Pepper
- ❖ Salt

Directions:

1. Add all ingredients into the soup maker and stir well. Seal soup maker with lid and cook on chunky mode. Season soup with salt and pepper. Serve and enjoy.

Tomato Soups

Tomato Cabbage Soup

Servings|4   Time|26 minutes
Nutritional Content (per serving):
Cal| 108   Fat| 4g   Protein| 3g   Carbs| 21g

Ingredients:

- ❖ 340 g of cabbage, chopped
- ❖ 410 ml hot water
- ❖ 1 vegetable stock cube
- ❖ 400 g passata
- ❖ 1g garlic, chopped

- ❖ 1 carrot, sliced
- ❖ 1 large onion, chopped
- ❖ 15 ml olive oil
- ❖ Pepper
- ❖ Salt

Directions:

1. Heat oil in a pan over medium heat. Add onion and garlic and sauté until onion is softened. Transfer to the soup maker. Add remaining ingredients to the soup maker and stir well.
2. Seal soup maker with lid and cook on smooth mode for 21 minutes. Season soup with salt and pepper.
3. Serve and enjoy.

Flavourful Tomato Soup

Servings|4   Time|30 minutes
Nutritional Content (per serving):
Cal| 96   Fat| 4g   Protein| 2g   Carbs| 16g

Ingredients:

- ❖ 475 ml vegetable stock
- ❖ 15 g brown sugar
- ❖ 790 g can tomato, chopped
- ❖ 3 g garlic, crushed
- ❖ 1 medium onion, chopped
- ❖ 1 ml olive oil
- ❖ Pepper
- ❖ Salt

Directions:
1. Heat the oil in a pan over medium heat. Sauté the added onion and cook until onion is softened. Add garlic and sauté for 30 seconds.
2. Transfer sautéed onion and garlic to the soup maker. Add remaining ingredients to the soup maker and stir well.
3. Seal soup maker with lid and cook on smooth mode for 20 minutes. Season soup with salt and pepper. Serve and enjoy.

Creamy Tomato Soup

Servings|6   Time|35 minutes
Nutritional Content (per serving):
Cal| 80   Fat| 4g   Protein| 2g   Carbs| 11g

Ingredients:

- ❖ 790 g can tomato, chopped
- ❖ 700 ml vegetable stock
- ❖ 130 g carrot, chopped
- ❖ 50 g onion, chopped
- ❖ 30 g butter,
- ❖ 9 g salt

Directions:

1. Melt butter in a pan over medium heat. Add onion, carrot, and 1/2 tsp salt and sauté for 5 minutes. Transfer to the soup maker.
2. Add remaining ingredients to the soup maker and stir well. Seal soup maker with lid and cook on smooth mode for 25 minutes. Serve and enjoy.

Parmesan Basil Tomato Soup

Servings|4   Time|30 minutes
Nutritional Content (per serving):
Cal| 223   Fat| 17g   Protein| 5g   Carbs| 16g

Ingredients:

- ❖ 400 g can tomato, diced
- ❖ 1g fresh basil, chopped
- ❖ 45g parmesan cheese
- ❖ 120 dl heavy cream
- ❖ 475 ml chicken stock
- ❖ 15 g flour
- ❖ 0.5 g dried oregano
- ❖ 1g garlic, minced
- ❖ 45 g carrot, diced
- ❖ 26 g onion, diced
- ❖ 30 g butter
- ❖ Pepper
- ❖ Salt

Directions:

1. Melt the butter in a pan over medium heat. Add onion and sauté for 2 minutes. Sauté the added garlic and cook for 30 seconds.
2. Transfer onion and garlic to the soup maker. Add remaining ingredients to the soup maker and stir well.
3. Seal soup maker with lid and cook on smooth mode for 21 minutes. Season soup with salt and pepper. Serve and enjoy.

Tomato Spinach Soup

Servings|4   Time|35 minutes
Nutritional Content (per serving):
Cal| 83   Fat| 4g   Protein| 2g   Carbs| 11g

Ingredients:

- 200 g can tomato, chopped
- 60 g spinach, chopped
- 1 celery stalk, chopped
- 2 carrots, peeled and chopped
- 0.5 g dried thyme
- 950m l chicken stock
- 1 garlic clove, minced
- 1 small onion, chopped
- 15 ml olive oil
- Pepper
- Salt

Directions:

1. Heat oil in a pan over medium heat. Add onion and garlic and sauté for 2-3 minutes. Transfer to the soup maker.
2. Add remaining ingredients to the soup maker and stir well. Seal soup maker with lid and cook on chunky mode for 25 minutes.
3. Season soup with salt and pepper. Serve and enjoy.

Easy Carrot Tomato Soup

Servings|4   Time|30 minutes
Nutritional Content (per serving):
Cal| 128   Fat| 4g   Protein| 2g   Carbs| 23g

Ingredients:

- ❖ 790 g carrots, chopped
- ❖ 950 ml vegetable stock
- ❖ 790 g can tomato, chopped
- ❖ 1g coriander powder
- ❖ 1 medium onion, chopped
- ❖ 15 ml olive oil
- ❖ 60 g fresh coriander, chopped
- ❖ Pepper
- ❖ Salt

Directions:

1. Heat oil in a pan over medium heat. Sauté the added onion and cook until onion is softened.
2. Transfer sautéed onion to the soup maker. Add carrots, stock, and coriander powder to the soup maker and stir well.
3. Seal soup maker with lid and cook on smooth mode. Season soup with salt and pepper. Garnish with fresh coriander and serve.

Healthy & Easy Tomato Soup

Servings|6   Time|20 minutes
Nutritional Content (per serving):
Cal| 36   Fat| 0g   Protein| 1g   Carbs| 9g

Ingredients:

- ❖ 790 g can tomato, crushed
- ❖ 110 ml carrot juice
- ❖ 5 garlic cloves, crushed
- ❖ Pepper
- ❖ Salt

Directions:
1. Add all ingredients into the soup maker and stir well. Seal soup maker with lid and cook on smooth mode for 15 minutes.
2. Season soup with salt and pepper. Serve and enjoy.

Roasted Pepper Tomato Soup

Servings|6   Time|1 hour 10 minutes
Nutritional Content (per serving):
Cal| 82   Fat| 3g   Protein| 3g   Carbs| 13g

Ingredients:

- ❖ 9 medium tomatoes, halved
- ❖ 710 ml vegetable stock
- ❖ 15 ml vinegar
- ❖ 15 ml olive oil
- ❖ 5 garlic cloves, peeled

- ❖ 2 onions, diced
- ❖ 1 large sweet red pepper, diced
- ❖ Pepper
- ❖ Salt

Directions:

1. Preheat the oven to 400 F/ 200 C. Place sweet red pepper, garlic, onion, and tomatoes on a baking tray. Drizzle with oil and vinegar.
2. Bake in preheated oven for 45 minutes. Transfer roasted sweet red pepper, garlic, onion, and tomatoes to the soup maker.
3. Add stock, pepper, and salt and stir well. Seal soup maker with lid and cook on smooth mode. Season soup with salt and pepper. Serve and enjoy.

Roasted Eggplant Tomato Soup

Servings|4   Time|56 minutes
Nutritional Content (per serving):
Cal| 144   Fat| 10g   Protein| 3g   Carbs| 13g

Ingredients:

- 2 large eggplants, sliced
- 2 g dried thyme
- 4 g coriander, chopped
- 3 g garlic, minced
- 790 g can tomato, chopped
- 15 g parsley, chopped
- 400 g can tomato, diced
- 950 ml vegetable stock
- 2 celery stalks, chopped
- 1 onion, chopped
- 15 ml olive oil
- 4 g cumin powder
- Pepper
- Salt

Directions:

1. Preheat the oven to 400 F/ 200 C. Place eggplants slices on a baking tray and sprinkle with cumin powder. Drizzle with oil.
2. Roast eggplant in preheated oven for 25 minutes. Transfer roasted eggplant to the soup maker.
3. Add remaining ingredients to the soup maker and stir well. Seal soup maker with lid and cook on smooth mode. Season soup with salt and pepper.
4. Serve and enjoy.

Artichoke Tomato Soup

Servings|4   Time|30 minutes
Nutritional Content (per serving):
Cal| 215   Fat| 14g   Protein| 5g   Carbs| 20g

Ingredients:

- 790 g can tomato, diced
- 950 ml chicken stock
- 400 g can artichoke hearts, drained and chopped
- 165 g garlic, minced
- 1 g dried basil
- 1.82 g dried thyme
- 1 onion, chopped
- 30 ml olive oil
- 125 g sour cream
- Pepper
- Salt

Directions:

1. Heat oil in a pan over medium heat. Add onion and garlic and sauté until onion is softened. Transfer to the soup maker.
2. Add remaining ingredients except for sour cream to the soup maker and stir well. Seal soup maker with lid and cook on smooth mode for 21 minutes.
3. Add sour cream and stir well. Season soup with salt and pepper. Serve and enjoy.

Herb Tomato Artichoke Soup

Servings|4   Time|20 minutes
Nutritional Content (per serving):
Cal| 183   Fat| 7g   Protein| 8g   Carbs| 27g

Ingredients:

- 790 g can tomato, diced
- 245 ml milk
- 0.5 g basil
- 2 g oregano
- 360 ml water
- 400 g can artichokes, chopped
- 30 g butter
- 1 garlic clove, minced
- 1 onion, chopped

Directions:

1. Melt butter in a pan over medium heat. Add onion and garlic and sauté until onion is softened. Transfer to the soup maker.
2. Add remaining ingredients except for milk to the soup maker and stir well. Seal soup maker with lid and cook on smooth mode for 10 minutes.
3. Add milk and stir well. Serve and enjoy.

Tomato Zucchini Soup

Servings|4   Time|40 minutes
Nutritional Content (per serving):
Cal| 119   Fat| 5g   Protein| 4g   Carbs| 19g

Ingredients:

- ❖ 1 medium zucchini, diced
- ❖ 1 g dried basil
- ❖ 1 g oregano
- ❖ 950 ml chicken stock
- ❖ 15 ml olive oil

- ❖ 5 garlic cloves, smashed
- ❖ 1 onion, chopped
- ❖ 4 large tomatoes, sliced
- ❖ Pepper
- ❖ Salt

Directions:

1. Preheat the oven to 218 C/ 425 F. Place zucchini, garlic, onion, and tomatoes on a baking tray. Drizzle with oil and season with salt and pepper.
2. Roast in preheated oven for 25 minutes. Transfer roasted zucchini, garlic, onion, and tomatoes to the soup maker.
3. Add remaining ingredients to the soup maker and stir well. Seal soup maker with lid and cook on smooth mode for 10 minutes.
4. Season soup with salt and pepper. Serve and enjoy.

Root Vegetable Based Soups

Cabbage Potato Soup

Servings|4   Time|35 minutes
Nutritional Content (per serving):
Cal| 233   Fat| 5g   Protein| 8g   Carbs| 41g

Ingredients:

- 90 g cabbage, shredded
- 400 g can tomato, chopped
- 400 g can chickpeas, rinsed and drained
- 540 ml water
- 1 potato, peeled and diced
- 1 green chili, chopped
- 1g garlic, minced
- 2g ginger, grated
- 1 onion, diced
- 3 g turmeric
- 1 g coriander powder
- 2g cumin powder
- 1 g mustard seeds
- 2 vegetable stock cubes
- 15 ml olive oil

Directions:

1. Heat oil in a pan over medium heat. Once the oil is hot, add mustard seeds and let them pop for 30 seconds.
2. Add onion, ginger, garlic, and green chili and sauté until onion is softened. Transfer into the soup maker.
3. Add remaining ingredients into the soup maker and stir well. Seal soup maker with lid and cook on chunky mode for 25 minutes. Serve and enjoy.

Creamy Squash Sweet Potato Soup

Servings|4   Time|30 minutes
Nutritional Content (per serving):
Cal| 175   Fat| 0g   Protein| 3g   Carbs| 43g

Ingredients:

- ❖ 795 g butternut squash, diced
- ❖ 335g sweet potatoes, diced
- ❖ 1 g ground ginger
- ❖ 1 g allspice
- ❖ 1 g cumin powder
- ❖ 1 g ground coriander
- ❖ 1g garlic, minced
- ❖ 480 g of water
- ❖ 1 small onion, diced
- ❖ Pepper
- ❖ Salt

Directions:
1. Add all ingredients into the soup maker and stir well. Seal soup maker with lid and cook on smooth mode for 21 minutes.
2. Season soup with salt and pepper. Serve and enjoy.

Vegan Potato Soup

Servings|4   Time|30 minutes
Nutritional Content (per serving):
Cal| 437   Fat| 28g   Protein| 7g   Carbs| 46g

Ingredients:

- ❖ 4 medium potatoes, peeled and diced
- ❖ 400 g coconut milk
- ❖ 950 ml vegetable stock
- ❖ 2 carrots, chopped
- ❖ 1 g dried rosemary
- ❖ 2 g dried thyme
- ❖ 15 ml olive oil
  - ○ g garlic, crushed
- ❖ 1 onion, chopped
- ❖ Pepper
- ❖ Salt

Directions:
1. Heat oil in a pan over medium heat. Add onion and garlic and sauté until onion is softened. Transfer to the soup maker.
2. Add remaining ingredients to the soup maker and stir well. Seal soup maker with lid and cook on smooth mode for 21 minutes.
3. Season soup with salt and pepper. Serve and enjoy.

Creamy Leek Potato Soup

Servings|4   Time|30 minutes
Nutritional Content (per serving):
Cal| 250   Fat| 7g   Protein| 5g   Carbs| 44g

Ingredients:

- 4 potatoes, peeled and chopped
- 3 leeks, chopped
- 60 g parsley, chopped
- 2 g dried thyme
- 0.5 g dried marjoram
- 950 ml chicken stock
- 30g butter
- 1 tsp salt

Directions:

1. Melt butter in a pan over medium heat. Add leek and sauté until softened. Transfer to the soup maker.
2. Add remaining ingredients to the soup maker and stir well. Seal soup maker with lid and cook on smooth mode for 21 minutes. Serve and enjoy.

Creamy Potato Soup

Servings|4   Time|30 minutes
Nutritional Content (per serving):
Cal| 219   Fat| 6g   Protein| 6g   Carbs| 37g

Ingredients:

- ❖ 875 g mashed potatoes
- ❖ 65 ml milk
- ❖ 410 g chicken stock
- ❖ 1/2 onion, chopped
- ❖ 14 g butter

Directions:
1. Melt butter in a pan over medium heat. Add onion and sauté for 2 minutes. Transfer to the soup maker.
2. Add remaining ingredients to the soup maker and stir everything well. Seal soup maker with lid and cook on smooth mode for 21 minutes. Serve and enjoy

Spicy Sweet Potato Soup

Servings|6   Time|30 minutes
Nutritional Content (per serving):
Cal| 143   Fat| 3g   Protein| 3g   Carbs| 28g

Ingredients:

- ❖ 680 g sweet potato, peeled and chopped
- ❖ 950 ml vegetable stock
- ❖ 2 carrots, chopped
- ❖ 10 g chipotle chili paste
- ❖ 2g garlic, crushed
- ❖ 1 onion, chopped
- ❖ 15 ml olive oil
- ❖ Pepper
- ❖ Salt

Directions:

1. Heat oil in a pan over medium heat. Add onion and garlic and sauté for 2-3 minutes. Transfer to the soup maker.
2. Add remaining ingredients to the soup maker and stir well. Seal soup maker with lid and cook on smooth mode for 21 minutes. Serve and enjoy.

Root Vegetable Soup

Servings|4   Time|30 minutes
Nutritional Content (per serving):
Cal| 129   Fat| 4g   Protein| 3g   Carbs| 23g

Ingredients:
- 450 g Swede, peeled and chopped
- 110 g parsnips, peeled and chopped
- 230 g carrots, peeled and chopped
- 3 g garlic, crushed
- 1 small onion, chopped
- 15 ml olive oil
- 2 g allspice
- 650 ml vegetable stock
- Pepper
- Salt

Directions:
1. Heat oil in a pan over medium heat. Add garlic and onion and sauté for 2 minutes. Transfer to the soup maker.
2. Add remaining ingredients to the soup maker and stir well. Seal soup maker with lid and cook on smooth mode for 21 minutes.
3. Season soup with salt and pepper. Serve and enjoy.

Healthy Celeriac Soup

Servings|4   Time|30 minutes
Nutritional Content (per serving):
Cal| 136   Fat| 1.2g   Protein| 6g   Carbs| 26g

Ingredients:

- ❖ 340 g celeriac, peeled and diced
- ❖ 185 g yogurt
- ❖ 540 ml water
- ❖ 2 vegetable stock cubes
- ❖ 4 g fennel seeds
- ❖ 1 potato, peeled and diced
- ❖ 1 onion, diced
- ❖ 1 leek, sliced
- ❖ 101 g celery, sliced
- ❖ Pepper
- ❖ Salt

Directions:

1. Add all ingredients except yogurt into the soup maker and stir well. Seal soup maker with lid and cook on smooth mode for 21 minutes.
2. Add yogurt and stir well. Season soup with salt and pepper. Serve and enjoy.

Chunky Vegetable Based Soups

Pasta Vegetable Soup

Servings|4   Time|35 minutes
Nutritional Content (per serving):
Cal| 191   Fat| 5g   Protein| 7g   Carbs| 32g

Ingredients:

- 75 g orzo pasta
- 540 ml water
- 2 vegetable stock cubes
- 400 g can tomato, chopped
- 4 g garlic, chopped
- 140 g frozen peas
- 2 g turmeric powder
- 1.5g garam masala
- 6 g curry powder
- 1 red pepper, diced
- 1 g chili powder
- 2 g ginger garlic paste
- 1 onion, chopped
- 15 ml olive oil
- Pepper
- Salt

Directions:

1. Heat oil in a pan over medium heat. Add onion, pepper, garlic, and ginger garlic paste and sauté until onion is softened. Transfer into the soup maker.
2. Add remaining ingredients into the soup maker and stir well. Seal soup maker with lid and cook on chunky mode for 25 minutes.
3. Season soup with salt and pepper. Serve and enjoy.

Flavourful Orzo Soup

Servings|4   Time|30 minutes
Nutritional Content (per serving):
Cal| 166   Fat| 5g   Protein| 4.2g   Carbs| 27g

Ingredients:

- ❖ 75 g orzo pasta
- ❖ 2 vegetable stock cubes
- ❖ 7 g curry powder
- ❖ 6g ginger, grated
- ❖ 1 small apple, cored and diced
- ❖ 3 g garlic, chopped
- ❖ 2 celery sticks, diced

- ❖ 1 onion, diced
- ❖ 1 carrot, diced
- ❖ 960 g of water
- ❖ 15 ml olive oil
- ❖ Pepper
- ❖ Salt

Directions:

1. Heat oil in a pan over medium heat. Add onion, ginger, and garlic and sauté until onion is softened.
2. Transfer sautéed onion, ginger, and garlic to the soup maker. Add remaining ingredients to the soup maker and stir well.
3. Seal soup maker with lid and cook on chunky mode for 25 minutes. Season soup with salt and pepper. Serve and enjoy.

Bean Veggie Minestrone Soup

Servings|4   Time|38 minutes
Nutritional Content (per serving):
Cal| 204   Fat| 2g   Protein| 10g   Carbs| 36g

Ingredients:

- ❖ 210 g mixed vegetables, chopped
- ❖ 7.2 g Italian seasoning
- ❖ 400 g can kidney beans, rinsed and drained
- ❖ 790 g can tomato, crushed
- ❖ 430 g chicken stock

Directions:

1. Add all ingredients into the soup maker and stir well. Seal soup maker with lid and cook on chunky mode for 28 minutes. Serve and enjoy.

Broccoli Lemon Soup

Servings|4   Time|33 minutes
Nutritional Content (per serving):
Cal| 202   Fat| 15g   Protein| 7g   Carbs| 15g

Ingredients:

- ❖ 1 1/2 lbs broccoli, chopped
- ❖ 15 ml fresh lemon juice
- ❖ 250 ml almond milk
- ❖ 500ml of water
- ❖ 22.5 g parmesan cheese, grated

Directions:

1. Add broccoli, almond milk, water, and half cheese to the soup maker and stir well. Seal soup maker with lid and cook on chunky mode for 28 minutes.
2. Add lemon juice and remaining cheese and stir well. Serve and enjoy.

Lime Sweet Corn Soup

Servings|6   Time|38 minutes
Nutritional Content (per serving):
Cal| 173   Fat| 4g   Protein| 6g   Carbs| 33g

Ingredients:

- ❖ 815 g fresh sweet corn
- ❖ 2 limes, juiced
- ❖ 3 g parsley
- ❖ 950 ml chicken stock
- ❖ 1 garlic, minced
- ❖ 1 small onion, chopped
- ❖ 1 small carrot, chopped
- ❖ 1 small potato, chopped
- ❖ 15 ml olive oil
- ❖ Pepper
- ❖ Salt

Directions:
1. Heat oil in a pan over medium heat. Add onion and garlic and sauté for 2-3 minutes. Transfer to the soup maker.
2. Add remaining ingredients to the soup maker and cook on chunky mode for 28 minutes.
3. Season soup with salt and pepper. Serve and enjoy.

Corn Veg Soup

Servings|3   Time|25 minutes
Nutritional Content (per serving):
Cal| 76   Fat| 4g   Protein| 1,3g   Carbs| 91g

Ingredients:

- ❖ 81 g sweet corn
- ❖ 6 g spring onion, chopped
- ❖ 15 g green beans, chopped
- ❖ 5 g carrot, chopped
- ❖ 14 g butter
- ❖ 15 g cornflour
- ❖ 720 g water
- ❖ Pepper
- ❖ Salt

Directions:

1. Melt butter in a pan over medium heat. Add corn, spring onion, green beans, and carrot and sauté for 2 minutes. Transfer to the soup maker.
2. In a small bowl, whisk together corn flour and 2 tbsp water and pour it into the soup maker. Add water, pepper, and salt to the soup maker and stir well.
3. Seal soup maker with lid and cook on chunky mode for 15 minutes. Serve and enjoy.

Mexican Corn Soup

Servings|4   Time|38 minutes
Nutritional Content (per serving):
Cal| 170   Fat| 15g   Protein| 2g   Carbs| 8g

Ingredients:

- ❖ 400 g cream of corn
- ❖ 30 ml olive oil
- ❖ 600 ml vegetable stock
- ❖ 45 ml salsa
- ❖ 7 ml vinegar
- ❖ 1 green chili, chopped
- ❖ 3 g garlic, chopped
- ❖ 1 small onion, chopped
- ❖ 20 g tomato puree
- ❖ 3 g red chili flakes
- ❖ 0.5 g dried coriander
- ❖ 1 g cumin powder
- ❖ Salt

Directions:

1. Heat oil in a pan over medium heat. Add onion, green chili, and garlic and sauté for 2 minutes. Transfer to the soup maker.
2. Add remaining ingredients to the soup maker and stir well.
3. Seal soup maker with lid and cook on chunky mode for 28 minutes. Serve and enjoy.

Spicy Cabbage Soup

Servings|6   Time|38 minutes
Nutritional Content (per serving):
Cal| 40   Fat| 0.2g   Protein| 2g   Carbs| 9g

Ingredients:

- ❖ 1 small cabbage head, chopped
- ❖ 30 g tomato paste
- ❖ 0.5 g thyme
- ❖ 2 g fennel seeds
- ❖ 9 50 ml vegetable stock
- ❖ 400 g can tomato, chopped
- ❖ 1 jalapeno pepper, chopped
- ❖ 1 onion, diced
- ❖ 1 celery stalk, diced
- ❖ 1 carrot, chopped

Directions:

1. Add all ingredients into the soup maker and stir well. Seal soup maker with lid and cook on chunky mode for 28 minutes. Serve and enjoy.

Cheesy Broccoli Soup

Servings|4   Time|38 minutes
Nutritional Content (per serving):
Cal| 426   Fat| 36g   Protein| 15g   Carbs| 7g

Ingredients:

- 320 g broccoli florets
- 30 g cream cheese
- 60 g butter
- 110 ml heavy cream
- 475 ml chicken stock
- 350 g cheddar cheese
- 110 g mozzarella cheese
- Pepper
- Salt

Directions:

1. Add all ingredients except cheddar cheese and mozzarella cheese into the soup maker and stir well.
2. Seal soup maker with lid and cook on chunky mode for 28 minutes. Add cheddar cheese and mozzarella cheese and stir well.
3. Season soup with salt and pepper. Serve and enjoy.

Cauliflower Broccoli Carrot Soup

Servings|4   Time|26 minutes
Nutritional Content (per serving):
Cal| 37   Fat| 0g   Protein| 2g   Carbs| 8g

Ingredients:

- ❖ 70 g broccoli, chopped
- ❖ 130 g carrot, chopped
- ❖ 130 g cauliflower, chopped
- ❖ 2 vegetable stock cubes
- ❖ 960 ml of water
- ❖ Pepper
- ❖ Salt

Directions:

1. Add all ingredients into the soup maker and stir well. Seal soup maker with lid and cook on chunky mode for 21 minutes.
2. Season soup with salt and pepper. Serve and enjoy.

Spicy Pumpkin Soup

Servings|4   Time|30 minutes
Nutritional Content (per serving):
Cal| 112   Fat| 5g   Protein| 3g   Carbs| 18g

Ingredients:

- ❖ 680 g pumpkin, chopped
- ❖ 950 ml chicken stock
- ❖ 2 g chili powder
- ❖ 1 g cumin powder
- ❖ 1 g coriander powder
- ❖ 1 g garlic, crushed
- ❖ 1 onion, chopped
- ❖ 15 ml olive oil
- ❖ Pepper
- ❖ Salt

Directions:

1. Heat oil in a pan over medium heat. Add onion and sauté for 2-3 minutes. Add garlic and sauté for 30 seconds.
2. Add sautéed onion and garlic to the soup maker. Add remaining ingredients to the soup maker and stir well.
3. Seal soup maker with lid and cook on chunky mode for 21 minutes. Serve and enjoy.

Chunky Broccoli Pumpkin Soup

Servings|4   Time|26 minutes
Nutritional Content (per serving):
Cal| 68   Fat| 1g   Protein| 4g   Carbs| 14g

Ingredients:

- ❖ 250 g broccoli, chopped
- ❖ 960 ml of water
- ❖ 2 vegetable stock cubes
- ❖ 2 g paprika
- ❖ 1 green chili, chopped
- ❖ 2 g ginger, grated
- ❖ 1 onion, chopped
- ❖ 116 g pumpkin, diced
- ❖ Pepper
- ❖ Salt

Directions:

1. Add all ingredients into the soup maker and stir well. Seal soup maker with lid and cook on chunky mode for 21 minutes.
2. Season soup with salt and pepper. Serve and enjoy.

Smooth Vegetable Based Soups

Creamy Mushroom Soup

Servings|4   Time|30 minutes
Nutritional Content (per serving):
Cal| 116   Fat| 4g   Protein| 5g   Carbs| 18g

Ingredients:

- ❖ 750 g mushrooms, chopped
- ❖ 480 ml water
- ❖ 475 ml vegetable stock
- ❖ 5 ml vinegar
- ❖ 1 g thyme
- ❖ 2 celery sticks, chopped
- ❖ 1 potato, peeled and chopped
- ❖ 16 g garlic, minced
- ❖ 2 onions, diced
- ❖ 15 ml olive oil
- ❖ Pepper
- ❖ Salt

Directions:
1. Heat oil in a pan over medium heat. Add onion and garlic and sauté until onion is softened. Transfer to the soup maker.
2. Add remaining ingredients to the soup maker and stir well. Seal soup maker with lid and cook on smooth mode for 21 minutes.
3. Season soup with salt and pepper. Serve and enjoy.

Cheese Broccoli Soup

Servings|4   Time|30 minutes
Nutritional Content (per serving):
Cal| 232   Fat| 14g   Protein| 11g   Carbs| 18g

Ingredients:

- 140 g broccoli, chopped
- 770 ml chicken stock
- 110 g blue cheese, crumbled
- 1 potato, peeled and chopped
- 1 cup leek, sliced
- 1 celery stick, sliced
- 1 onion, chopped
- 15 ml olive oil
- Pepper
- Salt

Directions:

1. Heat oil in a pan over medium heat. Add onion and sauté until onion is softened. Transfer sautéed onion to the soup maker.
2. Add remaining ingredients except cheese to the soup maker and stir well. Seal soup maker with lid and cook on smooth mode for 21 minutes.
3. Top with crumbled cheese and season with salt and pepper. Serve and enjoy.

Leek Mushroom Soup

Servings|4   Time|26 minutes
Nutritional Content (per serving):
Cal| 68   Fat| 4g   Protein| 4g   Carbs| 7g

Ingredients:

- ❖ 625g mushrooms, chopped
- ❖ 950 ml vegetable stock
- ❖ 90 g leek, chopped
- ❖ 15 ml olive oil
- ❖ Pepper
- ❖ Salt

Directions:

1. Heat oil in a pan over medium heat. Add onion and leek and sauté until onion is softened. Transfer to the soup maker.
2. Seal soup maker with lid and cook on smooth mode for 21 minutes. Season soup with salt and pepper. Serve and enjoy.

Creamy Mushroom Onion Soup

Servings|4   Time|30 minutes
Nutritional Content (per serving):
Cal| 90   Fat| 3.2g   Protein| 3g   Carbs| 14g

Ingredients:

- ❖ 10 mushrooms, sliced
- ❖ 15 g butter
- ❖ 5 g cornflour
- ❖ 1 chicken stock cube
- ❖ 2 g garlic, minced
- ❖ 1 potato, diced
- ❖ 2 small onion, diced
- ❖ Pepper
- ❖ Salt

Directions:

1. Add all ingredients into the soup maker and stir everything well. Seal soup maker with lid and cook on smooth mode for 25 minutes.
2. Season soup with salt and pepper. Serve and enjoy.

Simple Courgette Leek Soup

Servings|4   Time|30 minutes
Nutritional Content (per serving):
Cal| 157   Fat| 8g   Protein| 4g   Carbs| 21g

Ingredients:

- ❖ 2 courgettes, chopped
- ❖ 30 ml olive oil
- ❖ 700 ml vegetable stock
- ❖ 1 potato, diced
- ❖ 2 celery sticks, chopped
- ❖ 3 leeks, chopped
- ❖ Pepper
- ❖ Salt

Directions:

1. Heat oil in a pan over medium heat. Add courgettes, potato, celery, and leeks and cook for 5 minutes. Transfer to the soup maker.
2. Add remaining ingredients to the soup maker and stir well. Seal soup maker with lid and cook on smooth mode for 21 minutes.
3. Season soup with salt and pepper. Serve and enjoy.

Zucchini Coconut Soup

Servings|4   Time|30 minutes
Nutritional Content (per serving):
Cal| 128   Fat| 11g   Protein| 3g   Carbs| 8g

Ingredients:

- ❖ 400 g zucchini, sliced
- ❖ 120 ml coconut milk
- ❖ 709 ml vegetable stock
- ❖ 3 g garlic, minced
- ❖ 1/2 onion, chopped
- ❖ 15 ml olive oil
- ❖ Pepper
- ❖ Salt

Directions:

1. Heat oil in a pan over medium heat. Add onion and garlic and sauté until onion is softened. Transfer to the soup maker.
2. Add remaining ingredients to the soup maker and stir well. Seal soup maker with lid and cook on smooth mode for 21 minutes.
3. Season soup with salt and pepper. Serve and enjoy.

Cheesy Spinach Soup

Servings|4   Time|20 minutes
Nutritional Content (per serving):
Cal| 375   Fat| 35g   Protein| 9g   Carbs| 9g

Ingredients:

- ❖ 100 g fresh spinach, chopped
- ❖ 30 g butter
- ❖ 1 onion, chopped
- ❖ 2 g garlic, minced
- ❖ 120 g cream cheese
- ❖ 500 ml water
- ❖ Pepper
- ❖ Salt

Directions:

1. Melt butter in a pan over medium heat. Add onion and garlic and sauté until onion is softened. Transfer to the soup maker.
2. Add remaining ingredients except cream cheese to the soup maker and stir well. Seal soup maker with lid and cook on smooth mode for 10 minutes.
3. Add cream cheese and stir well. Season soup with salt and pepper. Serve and enjoy.

Healthy Spinach Soup

Servings|4   Time|25 minutes
Nutritional Content (per serving):
Cal| 190   Fat| 13g   Protein| 5g   Carbs| 16g

Ingredients:

- ❖ 400 g spinach, chopped
- ❖ 1 potato, peeled and chopped
- ❖ 125 ml heavy cream
- ❖ 1 L vegetable stock
- ❖ 2 g garlic, minced
- ❖ 25 g green onion, chopped
- ❖ 1 onion, chopped
- ❖ 30 ml olive oil
- ❖ Pepper
- ❖ Salt

Directions:

1. Heat oil in a pan over medium heat. Add onion, garlic, and green onion and sauté until onion is softened. Transfer to the soup maker.
2. Add remaining ingredients except for heavy cream to the soup maker and stir well. Seal soup maker with lid and cook on smooth mode for 15 minutes.
3. Add heavy cream and stir well. Season soup with salt and pepper. Serve and enjoy.

Almond Asparagus Soup

Servings|4   Time|20 minutes
Nutritional Content (per serving):
Cal| 233   Fat| 16g   Protein| 9g   Carbs| 18g

Ingredients:

- ❖ 600 g asparagus, chopped
- ❖ 150 g Almonds, soaked for 2 hours
- ❖ 375 ml vegetable stock
- ❖ Pepper
- ❖ Salt

Directions:

1. Add all ingredients to the soup maker and stir well. Seal soup maker with lid and cook on smooth mode for 10 minutes.
2. Season soup with salt and pepper. Serve and enjoy.

Celery Soup

Servings|4   Time|26 minutes
Nutritional Content (per serving):
Cal| 207   Fat| 18g   Protein| 3g   Carbs| 11g

Ingredients:

- ❖ 650 g celery, chopped
- ❖ 500 ml vegetable stock
- ❖ 1 g dill
- ❖ 250 ml coconut milk
- ❖ 1 onion, chopped
- ❖ 15 ml olive oil
- ❖ Pepper
- ❖ Salt

Directions:

1. Heat oil in a pan over medium heat. Add onion and sauté until softened. Transfer to the soup maker. Add remaining ingredients to the soup maker and stir well.
2. Seal soup maker with lid and cook on smooth mode for 21 minutes. Season soup with salt and pepper. Serve and enjoy.

Caprese Soup

Servings|4   Time|20 minutes
Nutritional Content (per serving):
Cal|445   Fat| 34g   Protein| 0g   Carbs| 44g

Ingredients:

- ❖ 12 basil leaves, chopped
- ❖ 500 ml chicken stock
- ❖ 600 g roasted tomatoes
- ❖ Pepper
- ❖ Salt

Directions:

1. Add all ingredients into the soup maker and stir well. Seal soup maker with lid and cook on smooth mode for 15 minutes.

Vegan Kale Miso Soup

Servings|2   Time|15 minutes
Nutritional Content (per serving):
Cal| 47   Fat| 0g   Protein| 4g   Carbs| 7g

Ingredients:
- ❖ 35 g kale, chopped
- ❖ 50 g green onions, chopped
- ❖ 2 g garlic, minced
- ❖ 35 g light yellow miso
- ❖ 1 L water

Directions:
1. In a small bowl, whisk together miso and warm water until smooth consistency Add all ingredients into the soup maker and stir well.
2. Seal soup maker with lid and cook on smooth mode for 10 minutes. Serve and enjoy.

Versatile Vegetable Soup

Servings|3   Time|25 minutes
Nutritional Content (per serving):
Cal| 103   Fat| 5g   Protein| 2g   Carbs| 14g

Ingredients:

- ❖ 65 g celery, chopped
- ❖ 60 g carrots, chopped
- ❖ 200 g potato, chopped
- ❖ 1 onion, chopped
- ❖ 15 ml olive oil
- ❖ 625 ml vegetable stock
- ❖ 1 g dried mixed herbs
- ❖ Pepper
- ❖ Salt

Directions:

1. Heat oil in a pan over medium heat. Add onion and sauté until softened. Transfer to the soup maker.
2. Add remaining ingredients to the soup maker and stir well. Seal soup maker with lid and cook on smooth mode for 15 minutes.
3. Season soup with salt and pepper. Serve and enjoy.

Garlic Corn Soup

Servings|4   Time|30 minutes
Nutritional Content (per serving):
Cal| 180   Fat| 6g   Protein| 6g   Carbs| 32g

Ingredients:

- ❖ 660 g corn
- ❖ 15 g olive oil
- ❖ 1.5L vegetable stock
- ❖ 1 shallot, chopped
- ❖ 6 garlic cloves, chopped
- ❖ Pepper
- ❖ Salt

Directions:

1. Heat oil in a pan over medium heat. Add shallot and garlic and sauté for 2-3 minutes. Transfer to the soup maker.
2. Add remaining ingredients to the soup maker and stir well. Seal soup maker with lid and cook on smooth mode for 21 minutes.
3. Season soup with salt and pepper. Serve and enjoy.

Lebanese Eggplant Soup

Servings|4   Time|35 minutes
Nutritional Content (per serving):
Cal| 109   Fat| 8g   Protein| 2g   Carbs| 10g

Ingredients:

- ❖ 1 medium eggplant; poke a few holes in the eggplant
- ❖ 750 ml chicken stock
- ❖ 3 g garlic, minced
- ❖ 1 onion, sliced
- ❖ 30 ml olive oil
- ❖ 0.5 g Italian seasoning
- ❖ Pepper
- ❖ Salt

Directions:

1. Preheat the grill. Place eggplant on hot grill and grill for 10 minutes. Turn every 2-3 minutes. Remove eggplant from grill and set aside to cool.
2. Once the eggplant is cook then peel and discard skin. Roughly chop the eggplant and set aside. Heat oil in a pan over medium heat.
3. Add onion and sauté until onion is softened. Add garlic and sauté for 30 seconds. Add eggplant, sautéed onion and garlic to the soup maker.
4. Add remaining ingredients to the soup maker and stir well. Seal soup maker with lid and cook on smooth mode for 15 minutes. Serve and enjoy.

Poblano Corn Soup

Servings|6   Time|30 minutes
Nutritional Content (per serving):
Cal| 131   Fat| 4g   Protein| 5g   Carbs| 22g

Ingredients:

- 550 g corn
- 250 ml milk
- 500 ml vegetable stock
- 1 g paprika
- 1 medium onion, chopped
- 2 g garlic, minced
- 15 ml olive oil
- 2 small poblano peppers, chopped
- 1 lime juice
- Pepper
- Salt

Directions:

1. Heat oil in a pan over medium heat. Add onion and garlic and sauté until onion is softened. Transfer to the soup maker.
2. Add remaining ingredients except milk and lime juice to the soup maker and stir well. Seal soup maker with lid and cook on smooth mode for 20 minutes.
3. Add milk and lime juice and stir well. Season soup with salt and pepper. Serve and enjoy.

Nutmeg Pumpkin Soup

Servings|4   Time|26 minutes
Nutritional Content (per serving):
Cal| 180   Fat| 14g   Protein| 2g   Carbs| 13g

Ingredients:
- ❖ 250 g pumpkin puree
- ❖ 0.5 g ground nutmeg
- ❖ 250 ml coconut milk
- ❖ 1 L water

Directions:
1. Add all ingredients into the soup maker and stir well. Seal soup maker with lid and cook on smooth mode for 21 minutes. Serve and enjoy.

Cauliflower Cheese Soup

Servings|6   Time|30 minutes
Nutritional Content (per serving):
Cal| 185   Fat| 19g   Protein| 2g   Carbs| 5g

Ingredients:

- ❖ 190 g cauliflower florets
- ❖ 750 ml vegetable stock
- ❖ 2 g fresh thyme, chopped
- ❖ 3 g garlic, minced
- ❖ 200 g cream cheese
- ❖ 125 ml heavy cream
- ❖ 30 ml olive oil
- ❖ 30 g butter
- ❖ Pepper
- ❖ Salt

Directions:

1. Preheat the oven to 425 F/ 218 C. Spread cauliflower florets onto the baking tray and drizzle with oil. Season with salt and pepper.
2. Roast in preheated oven for 10 minutes. Add roasted cauliflower, stock, thyme, garlic, and butter to the soup maker.
3. Seal soup maker with lid and cook on smooth mode for 15 minutes. Add heavy cream and cream cheese and stir well. Season soup with salt and pepper. Serve and enjoy.

Avocado Soup

Servings|4   Time|20 minutes
Nutritional Content (per serving):
Cal| 350   Fat| 25g   Protein| 22g   Carbs| 4g

Ingredients:

- ❖ 2 avocados, pitted
- ❖ 1/2 lime, juiced
- ❖ 3 g garlic powder
- ❖ 5 g fresh coriander, chopped
- ❖ 1 L chicken stock
- ❖ 200 g bacon, cooked and chopped
- ❖ Pepper
- ❖ Salt

Directions:

1. Add all ingredients except lime juice and bacon to the soup maker and stir well. Seal soup maker with lid and cook on smooth mode for 15 minutes.
2. Add bacon and lime juice and stir well. Season with salt and pepper. Serve and enjoy.

Almond Broccoli Cheese Soup

Servings|6   Time|26 minutes
Nutritional Content (per serving):
Cal| 284   Fat| 22g   Protein| 15g   Carbs| 4g

Ingredients:

- ❖ 250 g broccoli florets
- ❖ 125 ml heavy cream
- ❖ 375 ml chicken stock
- ❖ 25 g almonds, chopped
- ❖ 350 goat cheese, crumbled
- ❖ 6 g salt

Directions:

1. Add broccoli, stock, and salt to the soup maker and stir well. Seal soup maker with lid and cook on smooth mode for 21 minutes.
2. Add heavy cream and cheese and stir well. Garnish with almonds and serve.

Roasted Pepper Soup

Servings|8   Time|30 minutes
Nutritional Content (per serving):
Cal| 170   Fat| 10g   Protein| 5g   Carbs| 14g

Ingredients:

- ❖ 680 g roasted red bell peppers
- ❖ 1 L vegetable stock
- ❖ 1 onion, chopped
- ❖ 7 g cloves, chopped
- ❖ 1 cauliflower head, chopped
- ❖ 30 ml olive oil

- ❖ 230 g feta cheese, crumbled
- ❖ 1 g parsley
- ❖ 1 can tomato paste
- ❖ Pepper
- ❖ Salt

Directions:

1. Heat oil in a pan over medium heat. Add onion, garlic, and cauliflower and sauté until onion is softened. Transfer to the soup maker.
2. Add remaining ingredients except cheese to the soup maker and stir well. Seal soup maker with lid and cook on smooth mode for 21 minutes.
3. Add cheese and stir well. Serve and enjoy.

Creamy Cauliflower Soup

Servings|6   Time|30 minutes
Nutritional Content (per serving):
Cal| 170   Fat| 12g   Protein| 5g   Carbs| 11g

Ingredients:

- ❖ 600 g cauliflower florets
- ❖ 3 garlic cloves, minced
- ❖ 1 onion, sliced
- ❖ 750 ml water
- ❖ 125 ml coconut milk
- ❖ 1 medium fennel bulbs, chopped
- ❖ 15 ml olive oil
- ❖ 11 g sea salt

Directions:

1. Heat oil in a pan over medium heat. Add onion and garlic and sauté until onion is softened. Transfer to the soup maker.
2. Add remaining ingredients to the soup maker and stir well. Seal soup maker with lid and cook on smooth mode for 21 minutes. Serve and enjoy.

Coconut Garlic Mushroom Soup

Servings|5   Time|30 minutes
Nutritional Content (per serving):
Cal| 251   Fat| 23g   Protein| 5g   Carbs| 9g

Ingredients:

- ❖ 500 g mushrooms, sliced
- ❖ 250 ml coconut milk
- ❖ 250 ml heavy cream
- ❖ 15 ml olive oil
- ❖ 500 ml vegetable broth
- ❖ 5 garlic cloves, minced
- ❖ 1/2 onion, diced
- ❖ Pepper
- ❖ Salt

Directions:

1. Heat oil in a pan over medium heat. Add mushrooms and onions and sauté for 5 minutes. Add garlic and sauté for a minute. Transfer to the soup maker.
2. Add remaining ingredients to the soup maker and stir well. Seal soup maker with lid and cook on smooth mode for 21 minutes. Serve and enjoy.

Cabbage Coconut Soup

Servings|4   Time|30 minutes
Nutritional Content (per serving):
Cal| 150   Fat| 11g   Protein| 3g   Carbs| 13g

Ingredients:

- ❖ 1 small cabbage head
- ❖ 30 ml coconut oil
- ❖ 2 g cumin powder
- ❖ 6 g turmeric powder
- ❖ 2 garlic cloves, chopped
- ❖ 750 ml vegetable stock
- ❖ 60 ml coconut milk
- ❖ 1 g pepper
- ❖ 3 g salt

Directions:

1. Heat oil in a pan over medium heat. Add cabbage and garlic and sauté for 5 minutes. Transfer to the soup maker.
2. Add remaining ingredients to the soup maker and stir well. Seal soup maker with lid and cook on smooth mode for 21 minutes. Serve and enjoy.

Broccoli Avocado Soup

Servings|3   Time|20 minutes
Nutritional Content (per serving):
Cal| 90   Fat| 3g   Protein| 7g   Carbs| 10g

Ingredients:

- ❖ 300 g broccoli florets
- ❖ 500 ml vegetable broth
- ❖ 1 small avocado, peeled and sliced
- ❖ 1 g nutmeg

Directions:

1. Add all ingredients to the soup maker and stir well. Seal soup maker with lid and cook on smooth mode for 15 minutes. Serve and enjoy.

Soups Made from Poultry

Chicken Bean Soup

Servings|4   Time|38 minutes
Nutritional Content (per serving):
Cal| 350   Fat| 8g   Protein| 34g   Carbs| 36g

Ingredients:

- ❖ 450 g tomato passata
- ❖ 500 ml chicken stock
- ❖ 1 g Italian seasoning
- ❖ 360 g can butter beans, drained
- ❖ 1 onion, chopped
- ❖ 95 g soup pasta shells
- ❖ 2 chicken breasts, cooked and shredded
- ❖ 5 ml olive oil
- ❖ Pepper
- ❖ Salt

Directions:

1. Heat oil in a pan over medium heat. Add onion and sauté until onion is softened.
2. Transfer sautéed onion to the soup maker. Add remaining ingredients and stir everything well.
3. Seal soup maker with lid and cook on chunky mode. Season soup with salt and pepper. Serve and enjoy.

Red Bean Turkey Soup

Servings|4   Prep. Time|5 minutes   Cook Time|33 minutes
Nutritional Content (per serving):
Cal| 157   Fat| 6g   Protein| 16g   Carbs| 13g

Ingredients:

- ❖ 1 can red beans, rinsed and drained
- ❖ 500 g ground turkey, crumbled
- ❖ 1 g dried oregano
- ❖ 5 g chili powder
- ❖ 1 onion, chopped
- ❖ 100 g green chilies, diced
- ❖ 225 g can tomato, crushed
- ❖ 500 ml chicken stock
- ❖ Pepper
- ❖ Salt

Directions:
1. Add all ingredients into the soup maker and stir well. Seal soup maker with lid and cook on chunky mode. Season soup with salt and pepper. Serve and enjoy.

Classic Chicken Noodle Soup

Servings|4   Time|38 minutes
Nutritional Content (per serving):
Cal| 206   Fat| 9g   Protein| 22g   Carbs| 9g

Ingredients:

- ❖ 2 chicken breasts, diced into small chunks
- ❖ 150 g egg noodles
- ❖ 1 g dried rosemary
- ❖ 5 g ginger, grated
- ❖ 2 chicken stock cubes
- ❖ 1 L water
- ❖ 2 g garlic, minced
- ❖ 2 carrots, peeled and diced
- ❖ 25 g spring onions, sliced
- ❖ 2 celery sticks, sliced
- ❖ 15 ml olive oil
- ❖ Pepper
- ❖ Salt

Directions:

1. Heat oil in a pan over medium heat. Add chicken and cook until brown.
2. Transfer chicken to the soup maker. Add remaining ingredients to the soup maker and stir well.
3. Seal soup maker with lid and cook on chunky mode for 28 minutes. Season soup with salt and pepper. Serve and enjoy.

Tasty Chicken Vegetable Soup

Servings|4   Time|38 minutes
Nutritional Content (per serving):
Cal| 106   Fat| 3g   Protein| 12g   Carbs| 9g

Ingredients:

- 140 g chicken breasts, cooked and diced
- 1 ml liquid stevia
- 2 g coriander powder
- 1/2 lemon, juiced
- 3 g turmeric powder
- 1 red chili, sliced
- 125 g mushrooms, sliced
- 2 chicken stock cubes
- 1 L water
- 5 g ginger, grated
- 3 g garlic, minced
- 255 g butternut squash, peeled and diced
- 25 g spring onion, sliced
- Pepper
- Salt

Directions:

1. Add all ingredients except lemon juice into the soup maker and stir well. Seal soup maker with lid and cook on chunky mode for 28 minutes.
2. Add lemon juice and stir well. Season soup with salt and pepper. Serve and enjoy.

Chili Chicken Soup

Servings|4   Time|38 minutes
Nutritional Content (per serving):
Cal| 251   Fat| 10g   Protein| 18g   Carbs| 23g

Ingredients:

- 140 g chicken, cooked and shredded
- 800 ml chicken stock
- 30 ml lime juice
- 1 g cumin powder
- 1 1/2 chili, chopped
- 1 garlic clove, chopped
- 300 g tomato passata
- 1 onion, chopped
- 15 ml olive oil
- Pepper
- Salt

Directions:

1. Heat oil in a pan over medium heat. Add onion, garlic, and chili and sauté until onion is softened. Transfer to the soup maker.
2. Add remaining ingredients to the soup maker and stir well. Seal soup maker with lid and cook on chunky mode for 28 minutes.
3. Season soup with salt and pepper. Serve and enjoy.

Chicken Mushroom Soup

Servings|4   Time|26 minutes
Nutritional Content (per serving):
Cal| 167   Fat| 6g   Protein| 22g   Carbs| 5g

Ingredients:

- ❖ 2 chicken breasts, boneless, cooked and shredded
- ❖ 2 g garlic, minced
- ❖ 5 g butter
- ❖ 4 mushrooms, chopped
- ❖ 1 onion, chopped
- ❖ 1 small carrot, chopped
- ❖ 500 ml water
- ❖ 3 g cornflour
- ❖ 1 chicken stock cube
- ❖ Pepper
- ❖ Salt

Directions:

1. Add all ingredients into the soup maker and stir well. Seal soup maker with lid and cook on smooth mode for 21 minutes.
2. Season soup with salt and pepper. Serve and enjoy.

Turkey Bean Soup

Servings|6   Time|40 minutes
Nutritional Content (per serving):
Cal| 204   Fat| 8g   Protein| 19g   Carbs| 17g

Ingredients:

- 60 g baby spinach, chopped
- 280 g cooked turkey, shredded
- 250 g can cannellini beans, rinsed and drained
- 500 ml water
- 1 L chicken stock
- 1 g cayenne pepper
- 1 g oregano
- 1 g dried parsley
- 1 jalapeno pepper, chopped
- 2 carrots, peeled and diced
- 1 leek, diced
- 1 onion, diced
- 3 g garlic, minced
- 30 ml olive oil
- Pepper
- Salt

Directions:

1. Heat oil in a pan over medium heat. Add carrots, jalapeno, leek, onion, and garlic and cook for 5-6 minutes. Transfer to the soup maker.
2. Add remaining ingredients except turkey to the soup maker and stir well. Seal soup maker with lid and cook on chunky mode for 25 minutes.
3. Add shredded turkey and stir well. Season soup with salt and pepper. Serve and enjoy.

Thai Chicken Soup

Servings|4   Time|30 minutes
Nutritional Content (per serving):
Cal| 435   Fat| 31g   Protein| 24g   Carbs| 17g

Ingredients:

- 2 chicken breasts, boneless, cooked and shredded
- 3 g cornflour
- 1 potato, diced
- 1 onion, chopped
- 15 g butter
- 5 ml lemon juice
- 5 g Thai green curry paste
- 1 chicken stock cube
- 375 ml coconut milk
- 1 g coriander, chopped
- 5 g fresh basil, chopped
- 3 g garlic, minced
- 875 ml hot water
- Pepper
- Salt

Directions:

1. Add all ingredients into the soup maker and stir everything well. Seal soup maker with lid and cook on smooth mode for 25 minutes.
2. Season soup with salt and pepper. Serve and enjoy.

Chicken Sweet corn Soup

Servings|4   Time|30 minutes
Nutritional Content (per serving):
Cal| 182   Fat| 9g   Protein| 22g   Carbs| 4g

Ingredients:

- ❖ 2 chicken breasts, boneless, cooked, and shredded
- ❖ 15 g butter
- ❖ 25 ml soy sauce
- ❖ 500 ml chicken stock
- ❖ 3 g cornflour
- ❖ 1 g ginger, grated
- ❖ 3 g garlic, minced
- ❖ 85 g frozen sweet corn

Directions:

1. Add all ingredients into the soup maker and stir well. Seal soup maker with lid and cook on chunky mode for 25 minutes. Stir well and serve.

Delicious Asian Chicken Soup

Servings|4   Time|26 minutes
Nutritional Content (per serving):
Cal| 171   Fat| 6g   Protein| 22g   Carbs| 7g

Ingredients:

- ❖ 2 chicken breasts, cooked and diced
- ❖ 1 L chicken stock
- ❖ 55 g spring onions, sliced
- ❖ 10 g ginger, grated
- ❖ 3 g garlic, crushed
- ❖ 1 1/2 red chili, sliced
- ❖ 1 dried lemongrass
- ❖ 15 ml lemon juice
- ❖ 50 g Thai curry paste

Directions:

1. Add all ingredients into the soup maker and stir well. Seal soup maker with lid and cook on smooth mode for 21 minutes. Stir well and serve.

Cauliflower Chicken Soup

Servings|4   Time|30 minutes
Nutritional Content (per serving):
Cal| 300   Fat| 21g   Protein|23g   Carbs| 4g

Ingredients:

- ❖ 280 g chicken, cooked and shredded
- ❖ 170 g cauliflower rice, cooked
- ❖ 1 g onion powder
- ❖ 65 ml heavy cream

- ❖ 250 ml chicken stock
- ❖ 100 g cream cheese, cubed
- ❖ 10 g garlic, minced
- ❖ 30 g butter
- ❖ Salt

Directions:

1. Add all ingredients into the soup maker and stir well. Seal soup maker with lid and cook on chunky mode for 25 minutes. Serve and enjoy.

Chicken Taco Soup

Servings|4   Time|33 minutes
Nutritional Content (per serving):
Cal| 440   Fat| 32g   Protein| 30g   Carbs| 8g

Ingredients:

- 280 g chicken breasts, cooked and shredded
- 125 ml heavy cream
- 230 g cream cheese
- 1 g taco seasoning
- 300 g can tomato
- 15 ml olive oil
- 750 g chicken stock
- Salt

Directions:

1. Add all ingredients except heavy cream and cream cheese into the soup maker and stir well.
2. Seal soup maker with lid and cook on chunky mode for 28 minutes. Add heavy cream and cream cheese and stir well. Serve and enjoy.

Soups Made from Seafood

Asian Prawn Soup

Servings|4   Time|30 minutes
Nutritional Content (per serving):
Cal| 521   Fat| 8g   Protein| 94g   Carbs| 13g

Ingredients:

- ❖ 600 g fresh prawns
- ❖ 250 ml fish stock
- ❖ 60 g yogurt
- ❖ 1 lime, juiced
- ❖ 5 g ginger garlic paste
- ❖ 1 g paprika
- ❖ 3 g curry powder
- ❖ 1 g mixed spice
- ❖ 1 g coriander powder
- ❖ 1 small onion, chopped
- ❖ 1 red pepper, chopped
- ❖ Pepper
- ❖ Salt

Directions:

1. Add all ingredients into the soup maker and stir well. Seal soup maker with lid and cook on blend mode for 25 minutes.
2. Season soup with salt and pepper. Serve and enjoy.

Smoked Salmon Cabbage Soup

Servings|4   Time|30 minutes
Nutritional Content (per serving):
Cal| 250   Fat| 14g   Protein| 11g   Carbs| 21g

Ingredients:

- ❖ 1/4 cabbage, sliced
- ❖ 5 smoked salmon slices, cooked and chopped
- ❖ 2 vegetable stock cubes
- ❖ 1 L water
- ❖ 340 g potatoes, peeled and diced
- ❖ 1 g dried rosemary
- ❖ 1 garlic clove, minced
- ❖ 1 celery stick, sliced
- ❖ 1 carrot, diced
- ❖ 1 onion, diced
- ❖ 15 ml olive oil
- ❖ Pepper
- ❖ Salt

Directions:

1. Heat oil in a pan over medium heat. Add onion to the pan and sauté until softened.
2. Add garlic and sauté for 30 seconds. Transfer sautéed onion and garlic to the soup maker.
3. Add remaining ingredients except smoked salmon to the soup maker and stir well. Seal soup maker with lid and cook on smooth mode for 21 minutes.
4. Add smoked salmon and stir well. Season soup with salt and pepper. Serve and enjoy.

Delicious Haddock Minestrone Soup

Servings|4   Time|38 minutes
Nutritional Content (per serving):
Cal| 153   Fat| 2g   Protein| 5g   Carbs| 25g

Ingredients:

- 125 g courgettes, diced
- ½ pound haddock, smoked
- 1 g basil
- 150 g pasta, break into pieces
- 2 celery sticks, sliced
- 1 onion, diced
- 2 carrots, peeled and diced
- 400 g tomatoes, chopped
- 2 vegetable stock cubes
- 15 ml olive oil
- Pepper
- Salt

Directions:

1. Heat oil in a pan over medium heat. Add onion, celery, and carrots and sauté until onion is softened. Transfer to the soup maker.
2. Transfer remaining ingredients to the soup maker. Seal soup maker with lid and cook on chunky mode for 28 minutes.
3. Season soup with salt and pepper. Serve and enjoy.

Smoked Cod Potato Soup

Servings|4   Time|30 minutes
Nutritional Content (per serving):
Cal| 200   Fat| 12g   Protein| 8g   Carbs| 18g

Ingredients:

- 455 g potatoes, peeled and diced
- 4 strips of smoked cod sliced, cooked and chopped
- 2 vegetable stock cubes
- 375 ml water
- 125 ml milk
- 1 cup leek, sliced
- 1 onion, chopped
- 15 ml olive oil
- Pepper
- Salt

Directions:

1. Heat oil in a pan over medium heat. Add onion and cook until onion is softened. Transfer sautéed onion to the soup maker.
2. Add remaining ingredients except smoked cod to the soup maker. Seal soup maker with lid and cook on smooth mode for 21 minutes.
3. Season soup with salt and pepper. Serve and enjoy.

Curried Cod Cauliflower Soup

Servings|2   Time|15 minutes
Nutritional Content (per serving):
Cal| 45   Fat| 1g   Protein| 2g   Carbs| 10g

Ingredients:

- ❖ 500 g fried cod, diced
- ❖ 230 g cauliflower florets
- ❖ 3 g curry powder
- ❖ 2 g garlic clove, minced
- ❖ 1/2 onion, minced
- ❖ 310 ml water
- ❖ Pepper
- ❖ Salt

Directions:
1. Add all ingredients into the soup maker and stir well. Seal soup maker with lid and cook on chunky mode for 15 minutes. Season soup with salt and pepper. Serve and enjoy.

Haddock Asparagus Soup

Servings|6   Time|50 minutes
Nutritional Content (per serving):
Cal| 266   Fat| 23g   Protein| 10g   Carbs| 15g

Ingredients:

- ❖ 800 g asparagus, cut off the woody stems
- ❖ 750 g Haddock, smoked, diced
- ❖ 1 g dried thyme
- ❖ 1 g oregano
- ❖ 0.5 g sage
- ❖ 375 ml water
- ❖ 1 cauliflower head, cut into florets
- ❖ 4 ml lime zest
- ❖ 30 ml lime juice
- ❖ 250 ml coconut milk
- ❖ 1 tbsp garlic, minced
- ❖ 1 leek, sliced
- ❖ 45 ml olive oil
- ❖ Salt

Directions:

1. Preheat the oven to 400 F/ 200 C. Arrange asparagus on a baking tray. Drizzle with 2 tablespoons of oil and sprinkle with salt, thyme, oregano, and sage.
2. Roast in preheated oven for 20 minutes. Heat remaining oil to the pan over medium heat. Add garlic and leek and sauté for 2-3 minutes. Transfer to the soup maker.
3. Add asparagus to the soup maker. Add remaining ingredients to the soup maker and stir well.
4. Seal soup maker with lid and cook on chunky mode for 21 minutes. Serve and enjoy.

Spinach Cod Soup

Servings|4   Time|38 minutes
Nutritional Content (per serving):
Cal| 306   Fat| 2g   Protein| 21g   Carbs| 54g

Ingredients:

- ❖ 850 g cod, diced, stir fried
- ❖ 250 g tomatoes, diced
- ❖ 3 garlic cloves, minced
- ❖ 2 celery stalks, chopped
- ❖ 120 g baby spinach
- ❖ 1 L of water
- ❖ 1 g Italian seasoning
- ❖ 2 g fresh thyme
- ❖ 1 carrot, chopped
- ❖ 1 onion, chopped
- ❖ Pepper
- ❖ Salt

Directions:

1. Add all ingredients into the soup maker and stir everything well. Seal soup maker with lid and cook on chunky mode for 28 minutes.
2. Season soup with salt and pepper. Serve and enjoy.

Curried Zucchini & Salmon Soup

Servings|5   Time|26 minutes
Nutritional Content (per serving):
Cal| 122   Fat| 9g   Protein| 4g   Carbs| 6g

Ingredients:

- ❖ 925 g zucchini, chopped
- ❖ 350 g smoked salmon, diced
- ❖ 700 ml water
- ❖ 250 ml coconut milk
- ❖ 15 g Thai curry paste

Directions:

1. Add all ingredients into the soup maker and stir well. Seal soup maker with lid and cook on smooth mode for 21 minutes. Serve and enjoy.

Ham & Bacon Soups

Bacon Tomato Soup

Servings|4   Time|30 minutes
Nutritional Content (per serving):
Cal| 152   Fat| 8g   Protein| 6g   Carbs| 16g

Ingredients:

- 3 cans tomato (300 g), crushed
- 625 ml chicken stock
- 1 g Italian seasoning
- 1 large carrot, chopped
- 2 celery stalks, chopped
- 3 g garlic, chopped
- 1 onion, chopped
- 2 bacon slices, cooked and chopped
- 15 ml olive oil
- Pepper
- Salt

Directions:

1. Heat oil in a pan over medium heat. Add onion, celery, and carrot and sauté for 5 minutes. Transfer to the soup maker.
2. Add remaining ingredients to the soup maker and stir well. Seal soup maker with lid and cook on smooth mode for 21 minutes. Serve and enjoy.

Pea Bacon Soup

Servings|4   Time|30 minutes
Nutritional Content (per serving):
Cal| 239   Fat| 11g   Protein| 13g   Carbs| 24g

Ingredients:

- ❖ 390 g fresh peas
- ❖ 1 lemon juice
- ❖ 5 g fresh thyme
- ❖ 1 L chicken stock
- ❖ 2 g garlic, chopped
- ❖ 2 medium leeks, sliced
- ❖ 3 bacon slices, cooked and chopped
- ❖ 15 ml olive oil
- ❖ Pepper
- ❖ Salt

Directions:

1. Heat oil in a pan over medium heat. Add onion and garlic and sauté for 3-4 minutes. Transfer sautéed onion and garlic to the soup maker.
2. Add remaining ingredients except for bacon and stir well. Seal soup maker with lid and cook on smooth mode for 21 minutes.
3. Add bacon and stir well. Season soup with salt and pepper. Serve and enjoy.

Easy Ham & Broccoli Soup

Servings|3   Time|30 minutes
Nutritional Content (per serving):
Cal| 87   Fat| 5g   Protein| 4g   Carbs| 9g

Ingredients:

- ❖ 285 g broccoli, chopped
- ❖ 135 g, ham, cooked, diced
- ❖ 625 ml chicken stock
- ❖ 1 small shallot, minced

- ❖ 2 g garlic, minced5
- ❖ 15 g butter
- ❖ Pepper
- ❖ Salt

Directions:

1. Melt butter in a pan over medium heat. Add shallot and garlic sauté until shallot is softened. Transfer to the soup maker.
2. Add remaining ingredients to the soup maker and stir well. Seal soup maker with lid and cook on smooth mode for 15 minutes.
3. Season soup with salt and pepper. Serve and enjoy.

Parmesan Bacon Asparagus Soup

Servings|4   Time|35 minutes
Nutritional Content (per serving):
Cal| 90   Fat| 4g   Protein| 6g   Carbs| 11g

Ingredients:

- 850 g asparagus, trimmed and chopped
- 45 g parmesan cheese, grated
- 225 g bacon bits
- 0.5 g dried thyme
- 1 L vegetable stock
- 2 g garlic, crushed
- 1 onion, chopped
- 15 ml lemon juice
- 15 g butter
- Pepper
- Salt

Directions:

1. Melt butter in a pan over medium heat. Add onion and garlic and sauté until onion is softened. Transfer sautéed onion and garlic to the soup maker.
2. Add remaining ingredients except cheese and lemon juice to the soup maker and stir well. Seal soup maker with lid and cook on smooth mode for 21 minutes.
3. Add cheese and lemon juice and stir well. Season soup with salt and pepper. Serve and enjoy.

Brussels Sprouts Cauliflower Soup with Bacon Bits

Servings|6   Time|30 minutes
Nutritional Content (per serving):
Cal| 115   Fat| 8g   Protein| 4g   Carbs| 13g

Ingredients:

- 1 small cauliflower head, chopped
- 550 g Brussels sprouts
- 4 g garlic, crushed
- 225 g bacon bits
- 15 ml olive oil
- 1 onion, chopped
- 125 ml coconut cream
- 1 L vegetable stock
- Pepper
- Salt

Directions:

1. Heat oil in a pan over medium heat. Add onion and garlic and sauté for 2-3 minutes. Transfer to the soup maker.
2. Add remaining ingredients except for coconut cream and bacon bits to the soup maker and stir well. Seal soup maker with lid and cook on smooth mode for 21 minutes.
3. Stir in coconut cream and bacon bits. Season soup with salt and pepper. Serve and enjoy.

Creamy Bacon Carrot Sprout Soup

Servings|4   Time|30 minutes
Nutritional Content (per serving):
Cal| 138   Fat| 8g   Protein| 5g   Carbs| 17g

Ingredients:

- ❖ 2 medium carrots, chopped
- ❖ 750 g Brussels sprouts, chopped
- ❖ 3 g fresh parsley, chopped
- ❖ 225 g bacon bits
- ❖ 750 ml vegetable stock

- ❖ 1 celery stalk, chopped
- ❖ 1 onion, chopped
- ❖ 30 ml olive oil
- ❖ Pepper
- ❖ Salt

Directions:

1. Heat oil in a pan over medium heat. Add onion and sauté until onion is softened. Transfer to the soup maker.
2. Add remaining ingredients to the soup maker and stir well. Seal soup maker with lid and cook on smooth mode for 21 minutes.
3. Season soup with salt and pepper. Serve and enjoy.

Blue Cheese, Brussels Sprout & Ham Soup

Servings|4   Time|30 minutes
Nutritional Content (per serving):
Cal| 124   Fat| 6g   Protein| 6g   Carbs|15g

Ingredients:

- ❖ 750 g Brussels sprouts, chopped
- ❖ 15 g butter
- ❖ 135 g ham, chopped
- ❖ 30 g blue cheese, crumbled
- ❖ 1 L vegetable stock
- ❖ 1 leek, chopped

Directions:

1. Melt butter in a pan over medium heat. Add leek, ham and sprouts and sauté for 5 minutes. Transfer to the soup maker.
2. Add stock to the soup maker and stir well. Seal soup maker with lid and cook on smooth mode for 21 minutes. Top with crumbled cheese and serve.

Cheesy Bacon Cauliflower Soup

Servings|6   Time|26 minutes
Nutritional Content (per serving):
Cal| 140   Fat| 10g   Protein| 1g   Carbs| 15g

Ingredients:

- 350 g cauliflower, cut into florets
- 150 g cream cheese, cut into cubes
- 1.2 L chicken broth
- 225 g bacon bits
- 250 ml heavy cream
- 235 g cheddar cheese, grated
- Pepper
- Salt

Directions:
1. Add cauliflower, chicken broth, onion, pepper, and salt to the soup maker and stir well. Seal soup maker with lid and cook on smooth mode for 21 minutes.
2. Stir in cream, cheddar cheese, and cream cheese. Stir well and serve.

Conclusion

Congratulations on making it all the way to the end of the Soup Maker Recipe Book UK Cookbook: More Than 120 Delicious and Healthy Soup Maker Recipes with Easy-to-Follow Instructions. Nutritious Soup Recipes to Boost Your Immune System and Nourish the Soul.

Thank you for going through the book, I sincerely hope you enjoyed the recipes.

As I said before, a lot of time went into creating so many recipes and I really hope you're satisfied with the recipes provided.

I'm trying really hard to create the best recipes I can and I'm always open to feedback so whether you liked or disliked the book feel free to write on my email at deliciousrecipes.publishing@gmail.com. I always reply and love to communicate with everybody. If you didn't like the recipes you can reach out and I'll share another cookbook or two for free in order to try to improve your experience at least a little bit.

Thank you for going through the recipes, enjoy!

Printed in Great Britain
by Amazon

13734816R00091